WATER GARDENS

A FIREFLY GARDENER'S GUIDE

WATER GARDENS

EDITED BY DAVID ARCHIBALD & MARY PATTON

ILLUSTRATIONS BY MARTA SCYTHES

FIREFLY BOOKS

First published as *Water Gardens: A Harrowsmith Gardener's Guide* in 1990 by Camden House Publishing (a division of Telemedia Communications Inc.)

Third printing 1996

Cataloguing-in-Publication Data

Main entry under title:

Water gardens

(A Firefly gardener's guide)
Includes index.
ISBN 1-895565-96-0

1. Water gardens.   I. Archibald, David.
II. Patton, Mary, 1946- .   III. Series.

SB423.W37 1996   635.9'674   C95-933096-8

Published by
Firefly Books Ltd.
3680 Victoria Park Avenue
Willowdale, Ontario
Canada M2H 3K1

Published in the U.S. by
Firefly Books (U.S.) Inc.
P.O. Box 1338, Ellicott Station
Buffalo, New York 14205

Printed and bound in Canada by
Friesens
Altona, Manitoba

Design by
Linda J. Menyes

Front Cover Photograph by
Derek Fell

Back Cover Photograph by
Derek Fell

Color separations by
Superior Engravers
Hamilton, Ontario

Printed on acid-free paper

A FIREFLY BOOK

Acknowledgements

Water Gardens: A Firefly Gardener's Guide represents, in its finished state, the commitment and cooperation of many individuals. They include art director Linda Menyes; artist Marta Scythes, who prepared the illustrations; managing editor Tracy C. Read; editorial assistant Jane Good; publishing coordinator Mirielle Keeling; typesetter Patricia Denard-Hinch; production manager Susan Dickinson; copy editor Catherine DeLury; and associates Audrey Beard, Lois Casselman, Laura Elston, Christine Kulyk, Ellen Brooks Mortfield and Sara Perks.

Contents

Chapter One:
Old Pleasures Rediscovered

By Friedrich Oehmichen

We were proudly enjoying the sight of sunlight dancing over the little waves in our just-completed pond when, as if to assure us that the water would hold, a sudden splash announced that the first frog, a leopard, had already adopted it. Before long, two other frogs arrived – even more surprising, since we had rarely seen frogs in this relatively dry section of our property. It was remarkable how quickly nature accepted our very modest effort to create an aquatic mini-environment only 6½ feet wide, 16 feet long and 30 inches deep. ✑ We were still greeting our first frog when a small beetle plunged into the water at our feet. At first, watching the creature scrambling on the surface, we thought it had fallen in by accident. But to our amazement, the paddling insect was trying to get into the water, not out of it, and after a few turns, it succeeded in diving. It turned out to be a back swimmer, which, although it must surface occasionally to take in air, is perfectly adapted to life underwater. ✑ With each newcomer, our interest and enthusiasm grew. Thus, our disappointment was profound when, two weeks after filling the pond, we saw mosquito larvae wriggling all over the surface. Some goldfish would have finished off the larvae within a few days, but they are ferocious predators and would have upset the ecological balance. Another possibility would have been to wage chemical warfare, but this, too, was out of the question. The final option – which we took – was simply to empty the pond, flushing the pests into the lower part of the garden. The choice was not a difficult one to make, as we had planned to fill the pond with rainwater from the eavestroughs anyway. A small gutter lined with fibreglass and integrated into its surroundings with a layer of pebbles and flagstones now car-

The familiar bright blooms of water lilies make them a water-garden favourite.

ries the water to the pond. At the other end, an overflow outlet drains excess water to a birdbath and farther, to the site of a proposed, much larger turtle pond.

When the snow melted the next spring, the pond filled with rainwater according to plan, and again, we watched the influx of its inhabitants. The water striders were among the first to arrive, along with a variety of beetles and water spiders. The only residents we imported were some unhatched salamanders and five tadpoles from our irrigation pond. To our relief, we saw no mosquito larvae. Apparently, a suitable group of predators had established itself in early spring and left them no chance to mature. But the birdbath – which no bird ever used – nurtured dozens of mosquitoes; it was probably too small to interest any of their predators.

Toward the end of that summer, I was delighted to see a dragonfly – a ferocious larva hunter – laying its eggs on a rock just above the water line. This spring, I carefully planted some scirpus on the shallow side of the pond close to our "sitting stone" so that we can, we hope, witness the miracle of dragonfly birth. The dragonfly larvae need these herbaceous ladders to crawl out of the water when the time comes.

The birds refuse to use the small basin prepared for them. They prefer the shallow side of the pond, with its one-to-three-inch depth. Originally planned as a refuge for shallow-water-loving creatures and for the young to escape the unpredictable appetites of their parents, this side of the pond has become a major attraction among the birds, which form veritable lineups to get into it. As the pond is just below our bedroom window, we can, to our delight, watch them quite undetected, getting to know them and their bathing rituals.

The first recorded ponds in private gardens were equally full of life, complete with fish and waterfowl. The Egyptians, whose agriculture depended heavily on irrigation, were highly skilled in controlling and retaining water, and they applied their skills to the embellishment of private grounds as well. Egyptian drawings from around 1500 B.C. show the garden of a high official in the court of Amenhotep I. Surrounding a central pergola full of grapevines are four symmetrically placed rectangular ponds with surprisingly detailed symbols for fish, water birds and lotus blossoms.

The Greeks, however, who dominated cultural development in the Mediterranean thereafter, showed little inclination to enrich their lives with waterworks. They left such tasks to the Romans, the empire builders who channelled the riches of the Mediterranean, western Europe and part of Asia Minor into their capital. A social class came into being that could afford to build spectacular villas, where water became a centrepiece once again. Quiet pools reflecting the beauty of water-

Sculpture can add a striking dimension to any landscape. Here, the crane and the rushes provide a vertical complement to the lilies and the water's surface.

side sculptures, cascades and fountains added not only visual and auditory pleasures but a cool freshness to the surroundings on sultry summer days.

In the Middle Ages, when most of Europe was building its tallest and boldest cathedrals, water features played only a modest role – in small fountains, for example, and in decorated wells in cities and on castle grounds. It was the Muslim culture that created the most famous water gardens of the period, pools dominating vast courtyards with shimmering mirrors, as in the gardens of the Alhambra in Spain. Other gardens displayed beautiful, ornate fountains feeding complex systems of small canals that guided the water in and out of courtyards and adjacent rooms. Magnificent water gardens built in the same period in Persia and India are further testimony to the ingenuity and creativity of the times.

Earlier, during the Han Dynasty in China, about two thousand years ago, water was seen as the source of life, and it became the symbolic element for purifying heart and soul. It was natural, then, for the Chinese to make extensive use of water in their gardens, building ponds of stunning beauty, adding unusual rocks that rose out of the water to connect it with the sky and designing bridges so that their perfect reflections in the water complemented reality.

In Japan, where many aspects of Chinese culture and religion were adopted, water became an integral part of garden art in the Heian period, around 800 A.D. The Japanese added their own variations, however. When garden space was limited, they created gardens conveying the intrinsic qualities of water – in lakes, rivers, brooks and cascades that are composed entirely of sand and pebbles, a method still in use today.

The Japanese garden artists, most of 11

Oriental landscape techniques and philosophy have greatly influenced garden design.

them Zen monks, also developed a fascinating approach to integrating another element associated with water – stone – into the domestic landscape. At the water's edge, stones and rocks impart a natural appearance as well as contributing a beauty that is all their own. Stepping-stones leading across the water's surface in a carefully designed sequence allow intimate contact with the aquatic environment, as do zigzagging bridges that characteristically make their way across Japanese water gardens. Access to the water is an intriguing design problem, and today's water gardeners can draw much inspiration from the Japanese.

Meanwhile, during the Renaissance and the baroque period in Europe, water's decorative potential was perceived very differently. In a revival of the old Roman tradition, water once again began splashing down waterfalls, gliding through grottoes and gushing high into the air from more and more powerful fountains, sometimes from entire galleries of jets. Villa Lante near Florence and Villa d'Este at Tivoli, near Rome, are splendid examples. Later gardens in France and other European countries harboured waterworks even larger and more ostentatious.

But tastes began to change. Around 1700, descriptions of Chinese and Japanese gardens began to appeal to the English imagination, sparking a new outlook that evolved into a complete rejection of the formal and blatantly artificial. Water took on a new role in the landscaped English gardens of such grand estates as Stourhead, Stowe and Blenheim. Full of natural beauty, the gardens were highly romantic, designed specifically to invite visitors to follow winding pathways to surprising and lovely views. Water appeared as quiet ponds and lakes, small brooks, splashing rapids and cascades subtly integrated into the landscape.

Landscaping styles on the large estates did not directly inspire the design of smaller gardens, however. It wasn't until two centuries later that William Robinson's book *The Wild Garden* initiated natural gardening on a more modest scale. And Gertrude Jekyll demonstrated how to integrate wildflowers and perennials, small ponds, brooks and even bogs into the garden. The famous English herbaceous border was born; rock gardens provided a place for tender alpine plants; in the ponds, splendid water lilies flowered while goldfish darted among their leaves; and bog gardens flourished, bearing a rich array of water-loving plants.

It was a time of extensive plant collection. Explorers and botanists roamed the world looking for new and unusual plants for the English to grow and enjoy at home. Many plants from North America found their way into European gardens, some of them aquatic plants such as pontederia, calla and *Elodea canadensis*, which adapted so well in the Old World that it clogged ditches and canals.

A profusion of lilies, petunias, begonias, marigolds, nasturtiums and lobelia brings *life to a formal pond. Recent trends favour more naturalistic settings.*

In the early part of this century, style preferences began to shift back to the more formal. But now, the growing awareness of the dangers facing our environment has reversed the trend, inspiring interest in preserving some aspects of nature in our own backyards. Aquatic ecosystems are the easiest to re-create, even in small water basins on a balcony.

Most homeowners do not have a natural water source flowing through their property that can easily be dammed to create a pond. But methods of creating and operating small artificial bodies of water are so advanced today that almost any aquatic aspirations can be met on almost any site. Whatever the aspirations, some basic considerations must be kept in mind.

As a water installation is not an easily movable part of the garden, much care should be devoted to planning. While it will take some time, the planning phase – first on paper, then later on the ground, marking boundaries of the new pond with stakes and string – can be an entertaining and enjoyable challenge.

13

A frog immersed in a sea of duckweed pro-
vides ample proof that both plants and crea-
tures can thrive in the water garden. Care
must be taken to ensure winter survival.

Choose the pond's location with care. If a pool is to be the focal point of the garden, it should be both visible and easy to reach.

The water itself is a major consideration. You will need a primary source of water that is readily accessible. Rainwater from the eavestroughs is an ecologically sound source of water, although a supplementary source is a good idea, to help avoid problems in dry summers and to allow control of the water level. You will also need to plan for an overflow outlet to drain excess water away.

Another question is whether to choose a shady or sunny location. In general, aquatic plants perform best in the sun, but so do algae. A shady location not only will discourage algae but will be better for fish, if you want them, as they prefer cool water. But shade, too, has its drawbacks. Prevent leaves from falling into the pond, because their decomposition removes oxygen from the water – a particular prob-

lem in winter, as oxygen is necessary for hibernating animals. If you decide to build a shaded pond, remember that buildings make better neighbours than do trees.

Depth is another factor to keep in mind, as it is crucial to the kinds of plants and animals you want your pond to support. A pond that is 30 inches deep will support many, if not all, aquatic plants but will be far too shallow to overwinter frogs and fish. If they are to survive the winter, the bottom of the pond must be below the frost line. Here in Montreal, one would need to go five feet deep. Local builders will be able to tell you the frost depth in your own area.

In shallow ponds, fish and frogs have to be transferred to frost-free quarters for the winter, as do the more tender plants. In our case, we did not have space for a deeper pond. We knew that hardy water lilies would grow beautifully, but we have no fish. What we did not foresee was that frogs would find the place acceptable and stay, unaware that the water is too shallow for them to overwinter. We can't prevent them from coming to the pond, but we want them to survive.

There are ways of mitigating the effects of the cold to some extent, even in a shallow pond. A small heating unit will help, and an air pump similar to the kind used in aquariums will keep the water in motion and the oxygen supply fresh. Another way to minimize freezing is to lower the water level an inch or so after the first frost, let the pond refreeze and then lower the water again. The air trapped between the layers of ice will act as insulation.

Deeper ponds can be hazardous, especially where there are children. One possibility is to fence the pond – not a very attractive solution, perhaps, but many municipalities insist on it. A more appealing approach is to build a horizontal "fence" into the pond so that it lies a few inches underwater, preventing anyone who falls in from sinking deeper but allowing water, fish, frogs and plants to pass through.

A final consideration is the plants themselves. Even a small pond can be a self-sustaining ecological minisystem. To achieve it, you will need a variety of plants. While aquatic plants are, in general, very easygoing, it is useful to know something of their different habits and roles in the ecology of the pond.

The three aquatic plant groups are bog and marginal plants, submerged plants and shade plants. Bog plants, such as reeds and water iris, with their roots in the water and their large, dark green leaves above the surface, absorb nutrients from the water that are, to other pond life, excessive. They are the "cleaners." Submerged plants, the oxygenators, such as elodea, absorb the carbon dioxide from the water and, in the process, release oxygen, which is essential for the life of the pond. Shade plants, such as water lilies, whose leaves float on the surface, are needed to shade the water, keeping it

Care at the planning stage will result in a healthy, low-maintenance pond ecosystem.

cool and discouraging the growth of algae.

Ideally, you should have representatives of each type and, to accommodate them, a graduated bottom in your pool. Many water-edge and bog plants will grow in a container holding 12 inches of soil, the top of which is 2 inches below the surface of the water. Water lilies and submerged plants need 12 inches of soil that is 16 to 20 inches below the surface.

Provided you've taken care at the planning stages, your aquatic plants will give you very little trouble once installed. Maintenance consists chiefly of thinning overcrowded plants and occasionally adding fertilizer for your water lilies and lotuses. Other plants absorb sufficient nutrients from the water.

Friedrich Oehmichen, a professor of landscape architecture at the Université de Montréal, tends his own water garden and nursery in Oka, Quebec.

15

Chapter Two:
Design and Construction

By Douglas Gilberg

When we began constructing pools and ponds—both for ourselves and other people—nearly 10 years ago, we didn't fully recognize their value in garden settings. We knew that the water itself would be delightful, especially with a glorious collection of water lilies. We knew that we'd love the sound of water trickling or cascading into a tranquil pool. And we've especially appreciated our garden pools in recent droughty years when water in any form seemed even more precious and enjoyable. ✑ What we didn't realize was that we would have a symphony at dusk each night when the assembled frogs and toads tuned up for their evening serenade. And we didn't realize how very often we would gravitate to our pools whenever we needed a quiet moment. The still waters reflect the sky and double our pleasure in poolside perennials and shrubs. On the fourth of July, fireworks fountains were set off on the far side of our big pool while we sat with our guests on a stairway watching the colourful displays and their reflections. The adults were as enchanted as the children. ✑ We also didn't realize in those early years of pool construction how important it is to build correctly. Slight errors in design will become very apparent, as we discovered. One of the hardest lessons was a concrete pool that we built for my parents. We used an inadequate little level, a gadget that you put on 17

Created to provide visual interest, water gardens should be located where people can see and enjoy them from inside the house as well as from a poolside seat.

a garden hose, and to this day, it is all too obvious that it didn't work. Some two feet of concrete sit out of the water at one end, illustrating how very necessary planning is to the success of any garden water feature. It pays to think the project through, make notes and plan on paper before lifting the shovel. Once the hole is dug, lined and filled with water, it is pretty permanent. Today, a four-foot spirit level is a major tool in our pond-construction projects.

Planning

The planning process depends, first and foremost, on what you expect of your garden pool or water garden. What role will it play in your landscape? It might serve as a reflecting pool to enhance other plantings or as the focal point of a new garden area. It might be the means for growing water lilies, lotuses and a variety of other water plants. You might wish to have a

shallow reflecting pool that is little more than a skim of water at the edge of a patio or terrace. This is a good feature for people with small children, although it is still not entirely safe. Supervision is necessary, no matter what the depth of the pool. A lot of people, with no intention of raising plants or fish, are simply after the sound or the look of water in their outdoor living area, maybe just four to six inches deep, stretching out below a small waterfall.

Our pools are balanced water environments containing both plants and animals. In addition to a wide variety of floating and submerged plants, we have fish, snails and multitudes of volunteers—frogs and toads in tadpole form. A bonus is that the tadpoles eat algae while the adults are romancing each other with song. Once you decide what role your pool will play in the landscape, you can move on to other considerations.

The sun is something water gardeners

both fight and love at the same time. You need at least six or seven hours of sunlight each day for water lilies to bloom, but sun is what creates algae problems. They can be overcome in the long run by growing water lilies and other floating plants to shade the water surface and by including oxygenating plants – those planted at the bottom of the pond – to recycle nutrients in the water.

Plan to have about two-thirds of the water surface covered with water lilies, lotuses, water hyacinths or other floating plants. We use one bunch of oxygenating plants for every two to three square feet of water surface.

Keeping a pool looking attractive in the shade where there will be a great many falling leaves usually becomes more of a maintenance problem than most people want to tackle. However, if you really want a pool in a shady spot, you can always rig netting to catch the leaves each fall. It's important not to situate a pond under walnut trees because of the toxicity of the nuts and possibly the leaves. If a pond is not subjected to a lot of organic matter (such as leaves), you may not have to clean it for two or three years. However, if it is overloaded with fallen leaves, twigs and other debris, you will have to clean it at least once a year.

If the site is rocky, the choices are simple. You either blast a hole or take the easier route and construct an aboveground pool. You can build retaining walls with railroad ties. On hilly sites, you can use boulders or rocks for building up the downhill side of a pond.

We strongly believe that, in most cases, you will want a site close to where you spend the most time, where you can enjoy the pool every day. Integrate your pool into your outdoor living space, and it will reward you amply through the warm seasons. Once you've chosen a site, test it by outlining the pond with rope or garden hose so that you can see the size and position it will have in relation to the rest

Cyperus and most other aquatic plants grow in sun while providing shade for goldfish.

of the area. For a garden pond that will include water plants, plan to have it 18 to 24 inches deep and no less than 18 square feet in area. If you have the choice, opt for larger rather than smaller pools. You'll be glad you did once the initial work is completed.

Finally, check the drainage of the area surrounding the pool site. You don't want to have it in a spot that collects storm water from miles around. In some cases, it would be wise to raise the edge of the pool slightly to keep it from collecting runoff during rainy weather.

Excavation

Gardeners and those who want just ornamental fish will approach pool construction in very different ways. The fish keeper will probably want to get rid of all the excavated soil and have it hauled away. The gardener, on the other hand, 19

A protective layer of corrugated cardboard prevents puncturing of the pond liner.

of our ponds is 100 feet by 15 feet and would have taken forever if we had tried to excavate by hand.

When the hole begins to take shape, it's time to use a proper four-foot level strapped to a good, straight 2-by-4 that equals the maximum pool width, or half that width if the pool is very large. In the case of a large pool, you may have to put a grade stake in the middle of the excavated area to check the level of the pond rim. Put one end of the 2-by-4 on the grade stake, and run the other end to every part of the pool edge. Believe me, this will pay dividends when you fill the pool.

At this stage, you can construct shelves for plants at the water's edge. This can be a help, especially if you want to have a transitional shallow area in the pond. A planted shallow area around the entire pond can be a safety factor if small children are going to be around.

Before putting down the liner, check the entire excavated hole for sharp protuberances. Then use sand, old carpet remnants or even corrugated cardboard to line the walls and bottom. In the case of our large pool, with its straight sides and bottom, we used sand and half-inch Styrofoam insulation panels. A commercial pond underliner is now being manufactured that you might want to check out as to cost and availability.

If you plan to have outdoor lighting, filters or pumps for waterfalls or streams, install a power cable and safety backups at the time of excavation. We recommend having a licensed electrician do this work for you. Be sure to make careful note of where and how deeply the power cable is laid so that you can avoid problems later. Investigate using low-voltage equipment in the pool area for reasons of safety. Be sure that a ground fault interrupter is installed either in the fuse box or in the outdoor receptacle.

If you use filters or pumps, be aware that a slight nick in the liner is potentially dangerous. Another danger sign is an oil

sees the excavated soil as an opportunity to build berms and waterfalls to enhance the setting. Planted berms backed by trees can create illusions much like the mini-landscapes often found in Japanese gardens. Plan these features before you begin digging.

Digging the pond is the hard part. For an average-sized pool, about 8 by 12 feet, it will take one person a couple of weekends to construct it and set it up properly. But once a pool is finished, it's the lowest-maintenance feature in the garden. Once we've set up our water gardens and have them in good balance, they may require, at most, six hours of care each summer. Garden pools are very forgiving of human foibles such as vacations and irregular care.

Plan to excavate when the soil is easily worked – that is, neither too wet nor too dry. For large water-garden projects, we use our backhoe or hire a bulldozer. One slick on the water. Turn off the power at the source, and repair the fault.

Materials

Until recently, the only materials for constructing garden pools were concrete or puddled mud. Now, vinyl, polyethylene and Butyl rubber are available. These materials, along with improved construction techniques, make it possible for the layperson to do a creditable job of building a pool.

When you use these materials, you can finish, or "cope," the edges with sod, boulders, rocks, pavers or flagstones so that the pool looks quite natural in the landscape. You can even run some of the coping materials down slightly below water level – if your pool edge is a bit out of the water, no one will ever notice the mistake.

Here's a good trick to use if you wish to cope the pool edge with sod or low-growing plants such as creeping sedums. Place burlap on the edge of the pool over the plastic liner, and let it hang into the water. Place the sod on the burlap, and it will wick the water up to the sod.

Concrete. We no longer recommend concrete for constructing garden ponds. For a concrete pool to last, it needs footings, reinforcement and several solid inches of concrete. Even when the concrete has been installed and cured properly, it's not uncommon to find it cracking within a few years. Cracks in concrete ornamental pools, waterfalls and streams allow the water to siphon out, disrupting not only the pool but possibly the garden as well.

Preformed Pools. We used to believe that people would want preformed pools because they could see the shape and size ahead of time and then simply dig a hole and slap it into the ground. We soon learned that, in general, that's not true. You can spend big money on heavy-gauge fibreglass pools that are not deep enough for most needs; hardy water plants need a water depth of 18 to 24 inches. And

these heavy-gauge pools will cost about three times more than the equivalent polyvinyl chloride (PVC) liner.

Furthermore, if you use a fibreglass or moulded plastic pool, you must dig a hole that is precisely the same size and shape as the preformed pool. If you don't – and sometimes even if you do – the whole pool may buck and crack when earth settles after rain or winter frosts. The other big

Flexible pool liners of polyvinyl chloride offer a versatility lacking in preformed pools.

problem with preformed pools is that you don't have much flexibility with the finished edge. The lip is on top, and if you want coping, you must install it on the lip of the pool. This is not an easy job, since coping materials are often too heavy for the pool material. Nine times out of ten, you end up with a water feature that looks too much like what it is – a plastic pool stuck in the ground with some rocks around the edge.

Flexible Pool Liners. We strongly recommend the use of flexible pool liners for constructing garden ponds. They are flexible not only physically but also in application. Current flexible liners manufactured solely for this purpose come in black or brown, creating a far more natural look than can be gained with the lighter-coloured liners used for swimming pools. 21

Create marginal shelves 9 to 12 inches below the top edge of the excavation. The sides of the pond should slope slightly inward from top to bottom.

Make sure that the entire rim of the water garden is level. This is easily accomplished by setting a carpenter's level on a straight edge of lumber suspended across the excavated area.

Cut a 12-inch-wide ledge to accommodate marginal plants and poolside stones. At this point, it is wise to double-check all depth and levelling measurements. Remove or cover any sharp protuberances.

Drape a pond liner, warmed by the sun to increase flexibility, into the hole, leaving an even overlap all the way around. The weights holding it in place can be eased off as the water is added.

When the pond is full and the liner has been pulled into place, trim the excess liner, leaving a flap 6 to 12 inches wide around the edge.

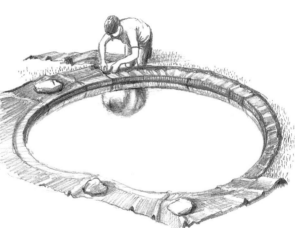

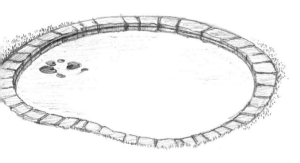

The pond is now ready for the stone edging or other coping. It is best if stones overlap the water's surface an inch or two to protect the liner from the effects of ultraviolet rays.

A waterfall brings appealing auditory and visual elements to the landscape. Once again, *the flexibility of PVC makes it an obvious choice to line both waterfalls and gardens.*

They also offer a number of alternatives for installing copings. Flexible pool liners are of three major types:

1. PVC liners with ultraviolet inhibitors are nontoxic and have a life expectancy of 10 years or more. PVC and Butyl-rubber liners are equally flexible, a consideration when pond plans are intricate. The smaller the installation, the more important flexibility is.

2. High-density polyethylene (HDPE), which is used to line toxic-waste dumps, is incredibly stable and nontoxic. An HDPE liner costs about one-third less than a PVC liner and has approximately the same life expectancy. HDPE does not have as much flexibility as PVC, so it will not fold as easily in corners and curves.

3. Butyl rubber liners, used primarily in Europe, now are available in North America. Some of the Butyl-rubber film has toxic ingredients that may leach into the water. Be sure to check this with the manufacturer or a professional pond installer. A Butyl-rubber liner has about the same life expectancy as a PVC liner. A

on the material chosen; for example, PVC liners are easily welded together with PVC primer and glue. HDPE liners are incredibly resistant to solvents, so you must use a recommended Butyl tape or heat-tack the seams with a high-temperature gun that can easily burn the material itself. I'd call in an expert to seal seams of HDPE or Butyl rubber – a leaking liner can cause many problems.

To estimate the size of the liner you will need, add two feet plus twice the depth of the pool to both its length and width:

Liner length = Pool length + (2 x depth) + 2 feet
Liner width = Pool width + (2 x depth) + 2 feet

The extra two feet will provide the allowance needed to anchor the liner.

Many liners are available in multiples of five feet (for example, 10 feet by 10 feet, 10 feet by 15 feet, and so on). Although tears in liners are the exception and usually result from abuse and negligence, it's a good idea to save some of the excess liner in case you need a patch at some future date. Larger pieces can be used to line small waterfalls or streams.

Once you have finished digging the hole for the pond, checked it for sharp objects and lined it with sand, commercial pond underliner or carpet remnants, you are ready to install the pond liner. Do this on a warm, sunny day so that the liner is warm and flexible. If it has been stored in a cool place, spread it out in the sun to warm up for about half an hour.

Spread the liner loosely over the excavation, making sure there is equal overlap on all sides. Anchor the corners with rocks or some other heavy objects. Begin filling the pool with water, and as it fills, pull and stretch the liner to eliminate as many wrinkles and folds as possible. Move the weights on the corners as the liner is pulled into the excavation by the water. The folds on the sides at curves and corners should be arranged as unobtrusively as possible. If heavy objects such as fountains, pumps, filters or plant containers are to be placed on the bottom, put cut-to-

further consideration is that, while Butyl rubber is very flexible, a 40-to-50-mil weight can create problems at corners and curves because of the thickness of the folds, and coping can be difficult to arrange over thickly folded areas.

The 30-mil PVC liners usually come in precut sizes up to 30 feet wide. You can get HDPE or Butyl-rubber liners in 20-foot widths up to 300 feet long. For larger ponds, you must seal or weld the joints on site, not always an easy task.

The method used to seal seams depends

Flat rocks used in streambeds and waterfalls should be slanted slightly downward to en-sure proper water flow. Too much current can inhibit plant growth in the pool below.

size Styrofoam panels under them.

Once the pool has filled, smooth the overhang and trim it to about a foot wide, pinning it down temporarily with four-inch nails. Now you can install coping. Be sure the edge of the liner ends with an upward turn so that water can't sneak under the coping and out of the pond.

Waterfalls and Streams

Waterfalls and streams can be wonderful contributions to the water garden, but once again, they must be carefully planned. A waterfall may be beautiful, but it can also dictate what else you can do with the pool. If you want to grow water lilies and other water plants, for example, design the waterfall so that it does not crash into the pool, creating turmoil and current. Pond lilies grow naturally in still water and eddies, away from strong currents. That is what you want to match in your own water garden.

The PVC liner has made the construction of waterfalls and streams almost foolproof. There are a few techniques to be aware of when building these water features. Basically, when you are using liners on waterways that go from one level to another, be sure to use a shingling technique; that is, each level of liner should overlap the one below it.

With both waterfalls and streams, be sure that any flat rocks you use are slanted slightly downward toward the next lowest level to encourage proper flow of water. When you stack rocks on top of one another, you can keep the water from being pulled in behind them by creating a series of steps, each of which has a piece of liner leading from behind it out and over the next step. The liner is, of course, covered with the rock slabs. This technique will bring the water forward over the edge of the steps, creating an effective cascade.

If you have a balanced water garden, it is not necessary to have either a pump or a filter. However, if you want a fountain, waterfall, cascade or tiny trickling stream, you will need a pump to lift the water. The volume of water and height of the lift are the two criteria that will decide the size of pump you need.

The sizes of pumps and filters depend upon what you want from them. It's best to double-check their technical specifications to make sure that they will do the job you want them to. Look at the catalogues and consult your local dealer.

If you buy a pump or filter that is bigger than you need, you can always restrict it at the output side with a restrictor clamp. Placing the clamp at the input side can burn out the motor.

Lighting

More and more water-garden electrical accessories are switching to low-voltage (12-volt) power, which is much safer. Submerged and floating pool lights of this type are now available.

We don't recommend underwater lighting for garden ponds. It just isn't very ef-

A "stairway" made of rocks and liner will ensure an attractive and functional cascade.

fective, since the water, even in the best-balanced ponds, usually is a bit too murky. A natural look is far more desirable.

Subtle, indirect lighting is often more effective than bright illumination. Besides, with too much light, you probably won't have as good a population of frogs, a delightful asset, to our way of thinking. Those nightly serenades are one of the glories of our water gardens. And the frogs do a splendid job of eliminating pesky insects, including mosquitoes, gnats and midges.

If you must have electrical lighting rather than the gentle effects created by candles, luminarias and tiki torches, we believe that backlighting and indirect lighting are most successful.

Establishing Balance

Once you have constructed your pool and filled it with water, you probably 27

The foliage of such plants as the hardy lily 'Pink Sensation' should cover two-thirds of the water's surface. In a new pond, allow water to stand a few days before adding plants.

should let it stand and mellow for a couple of days. If you're using public water, this is especially important, since it will allow the chemicals to dissipate.

Check the pH at that time. If the pH is over 7, you will have an algae problem regardless of how many plants you install. If you have a high-pH problem, a half-gallon of plain white vinegar diluted in about five gallons of water will lower the pH of 1,000 gallons of water by about one full point. Avoid changing the pH more than one point per day in an existing pond, especially if you have fish, as they cannot tolerate rapid changes. Once plants become established, they tend to regulate the pH themselves.

Now you can add the plants. Be sure to include oxygenating plants, because they are the key to keeping the nutrient cycle in balance. These underwater plants feed, through their leaves, on available nitrogen compounds in the water, which is how they compete with the algae. It would probably be more appropriate to call these "recycling" plants. Add enough lilies or other plants with floating foliage so that when they mature they will cover about two-thirds of the surface.

Wait about two weeks before adding fish to your water garden. During this time, or perhaps later, the water will go through a period of heavy algae bloom, often so severe that you can't see more than a few inches through the water. *Don't worry*, and don't drain the pool. Once the plants become established – submerged plants to take the algae's food and floating plants to shade the water – it will clear up. Be patient and do not interfere with this natural process.

We consider the plants the most important part of our water gardens. While we do enjoy the fish, we realize that they can create problems. The little two-inch koi, a refined carp, that you buy this year can

Bringing colour, life and grace to the water garden, fish also contribute to insect control.

Avoid overfeeding, as excess food sinks to the pool bottom and can create an algae problem.

become a foot-long bruiser by the end of the next year. And these big fellows browse on plants. They can devour your lilies and any other plant life that catches their fancy, although they usually won't cause a lot of trouble until they are over a foot long. In Japanese gardens, you usually don't see koi in the same pools as water lilies. Now you know why.

If you want fish in your water garden, choose slower-moving goldfish such as common comets; they will give you the least trouble. The main difficulty with fish is usually caused by owners, who tend to overfeed them. The extra food sinks to the bottom and rots, creating algae problems. With all the small insect and plant goodies that are in the average water garden, you don't have to feed the fish at all, but people like the way they learn to come to a handclap and a handout.

Douglas Gilberg, a specialty grower of herbaceous and aquatic plants, owns and operates Gilberg Perennial Farms in St. Louis, Missouri.

Chapter Three:
Management and Maintenance
By Henry Reimer

I n spring, a natural pond undergoes a remarkable series of meta-morphoses. As the water warms in the sunshine, algae grow, imparting an increasingly green cast to the pond. Frogs and toads lay their eggs, and tad-poles are soon hungrily devouring the algae alongside snails recently awakened from their winter sleep. Submerged grasses reach out, shading the pond bottom and providing shelter for newly hatched fish. Water lilies, cattails and myriad other plants begin to cover the water surface and fur-ther shade the water from the ever-increasing heat of the sun. ◯ Within weeks, a delicate balance reigns. Fish wastes and organic debris become food for plants and bottom-soil bacteria. Algae pass through the food chain to the fish. Snails scavenge decaying leaves and debris, earning them the well-deserved reputation as nature's sanitation engineers. Toad tadpoles soon complete their spring algae patrol, develop legs and leave the pond to feed on the burgeoning insect population, while bullfrog tadpoles remain to do the mopping up. ◯ Throughout the growing season, pond water nour-ishes the roots of nearby shrubs and trees, which in turn provide protection from harsh winter winds and allow a soft blanket of snow to insulate the pond from winter's cold. Each organism performs an essential function in the cy-cle of life. Caring for your water garden is simply a matter of maintaining 31

In spring, the brilliant pink 'Maggie Belle' lotus may be retrieved from its winter quarters and placed in the pond once the water temperature reaches 60 degrees F.

the conditions that will assure the continuity of the natural order of events. Common sense and an understanding of aquatic ecology guarantee success. Water gardeners in your area and local horticultural clubs are excellent sources of information.

Spring

In early spring, after the risk of severe cold has passed, pool coverings may be removed to permit the water to warm. As it warms, algae bloom will turn the water bright green, a natural process that will not harm plants or fish, so don't be alarmed. (Algae are discussed in some detail later in this chapter.)

Spring is the time to clean the pool. A small amount of silt and organic matter is quite acceptable, but you should remove heavy deposits. Small pools are generally less tolerant of bottom debris and require closer attention.

Fish that have hibernated in the pond will have exhausted their reserves of body fat and will be very hungry. Feed them when the water reaches 55 degrees F.

When the water has warmed to 60 degrees F, lilies, lotuses and other hardy plants may be moved from their winter homes and restored to their places in the pool. Divide and repot plants showing signs of overcrowding, and begin the fertilization schedule.

Before restocking tropical plants, wait until the water is 65 to 70 degrees F and all risk of frost has passed. Tropical lilies need a minimum night water temperature of 70 degrees.

While the ideal planting soil is well-rotted clay sod composted with aged cow manure, any heavy clay-bearing topsoil will do nicely. Sandy soils yield acceptable results but require more frequent fertilization in much smaller doses: the coarseness of sand permits rapid movement of nutrients from the plant container. Clay, on the other hand, binds nutrients and releases them slowly, acting as a nutrient bank from which plant roots can make withdrawals as needed. Commercial potting mixes are not suitable and should never be used. Whatever type of soil you use, be sure it contains no pesticide residues or road salt, which can be fatal to both plants and fish, even in small amounts.

Manures other than aged cow manure yield poor results. Horse manure has certain distinct advantages but requires considerable expertise and is best left to professionals.

For more details on planting and fertilization, see pages 50-51.

Summer

Summer duties are light, amounting to little more than minor housekeeping. To reduce the workload for the underwater sanitation department and to enhance the appearance of the pool, remove mature yellowing leaves and spent lily blossoms, cutting the stems close to the crown.

Water-garden plants, like the lotus (Nelumbo lutea), *attract beneficial insects.*

Prune plants often enough that one-third of the water surface remains open, allowing oxygen to get into the water and other gases to escape from it. If you prefer dense surface cover, be sure to provide some other means of aeration. A small aquarium air pump in a weather-resistant spot will do nicely. (Make sure the electric power supply has a ground fault interrupter.)

Debris falling from nearby trees or blown in by the wind should be removed. Willow leaves are particularly undesirable, as they contain a substance that is toxic to fish.

Feed fish sparingly several times a week, giving them only as much food as they can eat in five minutes. Excess food will sink to the bottom where it can accumulate and contribute to algae growth.

Fall

As summer turns into fall, hardy lilies begin to bloom less frequently and new leaf growth is scarce. The plants are approaching their dormant period, necessary if they are to bloom the next year. Dormancy is governed by the number of daylight hours and proceeds even if the water remains warm. Other hardy plants 33

Irises, shown above with swamp milkweed, boast exceptionally hardy root systems.

will show the same tendency.

Trim back dead and dying foliage on hardy plants, and move them into deeper parts of the pool so that roots are below the frost line. Roots of hardy lilies and lotuses can also be taken indoors for the winter (see pages 51-52). Leave the apparently lifeless stems of cattails (*Typha*) where they are above the water, for they conduct oxygen to the dormant roots, which will die without this pipeline. Cattail roots are hardy and can freeze solidly without harm. Yellow water iris (*Iris pseudacorus*) and blue iris (*Iris versicolor*) are also quite indifferent to root freezing.

Tropical plants will flourish until sharp frost or cold water kills them. To overwinter them, move them to greenhouse tanks or other appropriate areas before cold weather causes permanent damage.

The best way to keep falling leaves out of the pool is to cover it with protective screening. It is important to keep the pool as free as possible of leaves and other debris. As the water temperature falls, the snails become less active, and any sudden overload of organic matter will cause a population explosion of anaerobic (without oxygen) bacteria on the pool bottom. Their by-products include marsh gas — which is primarily methane — and hydrogen sulphide, both of which are toxic to fish. An ice covering compounds the problem: oxygen levels drop severely and gas levels increase, until fish mortality is inevitable.

It is advisable to transfer valuable or favourite fish to indoor aquariums where you know they are safe and where you can enjoy them year-round.

Winter

An experience of my own provides an excellent illustration of both the need for and the nature of winter pond protection. During a winter of high winds and heavy snowfall, a water line buried six feet below the driveway froze, requiring herculean efforts to restore service. As we had kept the driveway clear of snow, it was exposed all winter to prevailing winds and cold. On the opposite side of the house, however, we had allowed heavy drifts to cover the vegetable garden, and the next spring, I found firm, edible potatoes there. The snow, acting as insulation, had kept them from freezing.

One of the most successful methods of protecting your pond from the ravages of winter is also one of the oldest. First, remove all decaying organic matter from the bottom of the pool, then cover the pool with old boards, leaving a generous airspace above the water. Add insulation by piling on top of the boards a heavy covering of leaves or straw in garbage bags. The bags will simplify spring cleanup and keep the leaves dry, thus preserving their insulating quality. Be sure that the insulation extends beyond the pool border so that it will reduce ground-frost penetra-

The foliage of water lettuce (Pistia stratiotes) *provides shade that inhibits the growth of algae. The plant feeds on the same nutrients as algae, further aiding in control.*

tion. Snow fencing or other snow-trapping devices will provide additional protection.

Alternative winter protection involves a pool-heating system arranged to keep a few square inches of water surface open, permitting noxious gases to exit and oxygen to enter. Do not break the ice with a hammer or other heavy object; the shock waves will kill fish, and the sharp-edged ice may perforate the liner.

Algae and Green Water

Even experienced water gardeners are frequently alarmed as the water in their garden pools turns a vivid green in spring. Green water, or algae bloom, is almost inevitable early in the season or after a pool has been drained and refilled.

Sunlight, warm water and dissolved minerals, a major nutrient source for algae, combine each spring to generate an effusion of algae in pools and ponds. How-ever, as the plants – such as submerged grasses, water lilies, water hyacinths and water lettuce – begin to grow, they compete with the algae for the same nutrients and increasingly shade the water's surface and the pool bottom. Eventually, deprived of food and sunlight, the algae die and sink to the bottom, and the water will clear, sometimes in a few weeks and sometimes almost overnight.

Summer algae blooms are usually a sign of organic pollution from any of a number of sources: you may be overfertilizing or need to change your fertilization technique; excessive fish feeding can also contribute to the problem, because unconsumed food decomposes and fouls the water; insufficient plant cover will allow too much sunlight to enter the water; and finally, overstocking with fish adversely affects water quality. Fish wastes break down into nitrites and nitrates, which are prime food sources for algae and encour- 35

The stunning red blossoms of the aptly named cardinal flower (Lobelia cardinalis) *will bloom more reliably if good water quality is maintained in the pond.*

age their growth. Further, the breakdown consumes large amounts of oxygen, encouraging the growth of anaerobic bacteria at the pool bottom. The bacteria, in turn, produce toxic gases.

Another indicator of organic pollution is hairnet algae, or blanket weed, a stringy green mess that sometimes floats to the surface, where it gives the water a frothy, scummy appearance. It is more unsightly than harmful, but it should be removed. A stick turned round and round in it will wind the algae into a manageable ball.

This is, however, only symptomatic relief. The cause must be found and rectified. Again, lack of surface cover, overfertilization, excessive fish feeding and overstocking are all possible culprits. Surface water entering the pool will also contribute to the problem.

Very occasionally, and even more disconcerting, a grey-brown discoloration of the water may develop. If agitated, the water will have a putrid odour. This is another sign of organic pollution, and it usually appears when there is too much

Frogs are not on the list of water plants' natural enemies. In fact, the amphibians help *the water gardener by devouring insects harmful to the pond's inhabitants.*

surface cover and an undue amount of organic matter at the pool bottom, where anaerobic bacteria are flourishing. Restoring surface cover to normal and introducing aeration will quickly bring the situation back to normal.

Mosslike algae on the sides of the pool are harmless and, in concrete pools, beneficial, as they provide a cushion for fish swimming along the edges, reducing the risk of scrapes and abrasions. The undersides of lily pads frequently have a mosslike covering as well, which is not only harmless but is also a food source for tadpoles and snails.

Four basic rules apply in coping with algae and green water:
• Do not change the water. Fresh water will only supply the algae with a new source of dissolved mineral nutrients.
• Do not use chemical algicides. They merely postpone the inevitable and may damage fish and desirable plants. Using

them will also void most aquatic nursery warranties.
• Be sure plant cover is adequate for surface shading and bottom growth.
• Be patient. Establishing an ecological balance in the pond takes time.

If water problems persist, seek the advice of an aquatic nursery.

Pests

Aquatic plants have many natural enemies: moose, deer, beavers, muskrats, raccoons, turtles, crayfish, insects, large waterfowl and fish over 10 inches long. Fortunately, you will rarely encounter most of them.

Muskrats and crayfish are most often found in natural ponds and are known to eat plant tubers and fresh growth. They also burrow, causing banks and dams to collapse. Turtles and large fish graze fresh plant growth. Cover the plants with wire

A rubyspot damselfly perches gracefully on the tiny white blossoms of an arrowhead. A relative of the dragonfly, it helps control summertime mosquito infestations.

mesh or remove the offenders. Raccoons engage in generally obnoxious behaviour. While attempting to catch fish, snails and frogs, they often disturb plants.

Insect pests also appear. They rarely do permanent damage to healthy plants, but a lot of insect activity detracts from the pool's appearance. Fortunately, control is not usually difficult.

Aphids are the most frequent insect nuisances. You can dislodge them from the leaves with a strong spray from a garden hose; once they're in the water, the fish will cheerfully eat them. Aphids also have such natural predators as dragonflies and ladybugs.

Leaf cutter moths lay eggs on the underside of lily pads, and the larvae will construct protective cases by cutting circular pieces from the pad. Their activities are unsightly but not harmful unless the infestation is severe. You can control them by removing damaged leaves and the larval cases. In severe infestations, biological control is possible using *Bacillus thuringiensis* (Bt), a bacterium that destroys the larvae.

Random tracks across the lily pads mark the feeding paths of leaf miners. Fish, if you have any, will usually keep leaf miners in check; remove and destroy damaged leaves. In severe infestations, Bt may help to some extent.

Caddis fly larvae, which build cylindrical or cone-shaped cases out of vegetable matter, may damage fresh plant growth. Fish regard them as a delicacy, however, and even if you have no fish, they do not usually cause serious trouble.

Last but not least – the ubiquitous mosquito. Its journey to the pool surface frequently ends in the mouth of a hungry fish. Should a mosquito succeed in laying eggs, fish will rapidly dispense with floating egg rafts or wriggling larvae.

A small light installed near ground level

at the poolside will attract moths and other insects, and resident frogs will quickly learn to find their midnight snacks there. Many water gardeners rightly claim that mosquitoes and other insects are relatively scarce where there is a pond. As well, bird populations tend to increase when a source of water is available, depleting local insect numbers even further.

Fish Ailments

Fish problems, usually linked to unsanitary conditions and stress, are easily avoided. Oxygen depletion and rapid changes in water temperature, pH and dissolved mineral content will all stress fish, as will marked changes in fish routines, such as netting and transfer from one pool to another if rough handling is involved. Fish stress leads to depression of the natural immune system, which then permits fungal and bacterial infections to gain a foothold.

If fish feeding or swimming habits change, watch them closely. The most common signs of trouble are white spots on the fish, an infection known as "ick" (ichthyophthirius). Medications available at aquarium-supply stores are very effective if applied promptly.

An excessive fish population will give rise to a great many pool-sanitation problems. One inch of fish to five gallons of water is generally regarded as a maximum. Fish waste is very high in ammonia and passes through various stages of decomposition. Great quantities of oxygen are used in converting the waste into nitrite and finally nitrate form. At all stages, it is a prime food source for algae and bacteria. When the pool-sanitation system becomes overloaded, toxic gases from the burgeoning population of anaerobic bacteria aggravate the situation. Blue-green algae may proliferate and release oils that film the water surface. The oils inhibit the exchange of gases and nitrates, completing an unpleasant cycle of events. Anaero-

bic bacteria thrive in the oxygen-depleted bottom sediment, and toxic gases build up in the water. Fish are severely stressed under these conditions, and disease or death is unavoidable unless the chain of events is quickly broken.

Introducing new fish to an existing population may bring bacteria to which the existing fish have little immunity. Aquatic nurseries and aquarium-supply centres

The colourful and hardy koi are among the most popular of water-garden fish species.

are reputation-conscious and would not knowingly sell diseased fish, but if you are concerned, quarantine the new arrivals for a week or two.

Water is home to some of the most spectacular natural phenomena on the planet, making a pond an exciting, exotic addition to the home landscape. With a basic understanding of aquatic life and a minimum of maintenance, one can enjoy colourful blooms on the pool's surface, tall marginal plants swaying in the breeze and fish darting about fernlike floating species, as well as the soothing, refreshing qualities of the main ingredient itself – water.

Henry and Carole Reimer own and operate Reimer Waterscapes near Tillsonburg, Ontario, where they propagate over 100 varieties of aquatic plants on site. 39

Chapter Four:
Contained Pleasures
By Jennifer Bennett

W hen an old livestock trough came up for bidding at a local auction, most buyers waited for something better to show up; they were tempted by the usual antique dovetail dressers and quaint coal-oil lamps. But Mabel Heyd and Chris Santos recognized the potential of the old piece of farm equipment. The trough "was very appealing in a weatherbeaten way," says Heyd. "It was made of two planks about two inches thick. The wood was a lively light grey, and the hardware at each end was old but solid. It measured 70 inches by 28 inches by 18 inches deep and tapered toward the base. Nobody seemed to want it very much, and the bidding was not brisk. We got it for $10 on the third bid." ❧ What Heyd and Santos bought for the price of a fast-food lunch was not so much a former trough but a potential water garden in miniature – a small-time, much less labour-intensive version of the real, in-ground thing. When the couple rinsed out their auction find, "It leaked terribly, so we stapled 6-mil black plastic to the inside, and it holds water very well now." It also holds one water hyacinth, two water lettuces, three giant duckweeds, three upright bog plants (a blue-flowered pickerel rush, an umbrella palm and a giant water canna), four prostrate bog plants whose leaves float on the water, and two underwater oxygenating plants (an elodea and a sagittaria). The couple also put 41 in eight goldfish, 10 snails and the hardy water lily 'Rose Arey,' which "produced beautiful pale pink, six-inch lilies one after the other at three- or four-day intervals, except for one very cold spell in mid-June. We are also very fond of dainty Rosey's scent."

Such a small aboveground pond is remarkable but nothing new. In *New Improvements of Planting and Gardening* of 1717, Richard Bradley directed his readers to "cause some troughs of wood to be made, of oaken boards, about two inches thick; such cases should be six foot long, two foot wide at the bottom and two foot and a half deep, if they are for large plants that grow under water, or shal-

Container water gardens can be of almost any size, shape and material.

lower for such as do not require deep waters; the corners and other joints of such cases should be strengthen'd with iron, the insides well pitch'd and the outsides painted." Pitch was one of the pond-lining predecessors of today's polyethylene. Another was lead sheeting, which Philip Miller admitted in his 1731 *Gardener's Dictionary* made such gardens prohibitively expensive.

A trough is not the only kind of container that can be used for a miniature water garden, however. A gardener could fashion something similar out of wood or concrete pressed over chicken wire, then lined with polyethylene or a special pool liner – the liner is necessary not only to make the container securely watertight but also to keep any harmful substances in it from contaminating the pond water. Ready-made containers of many shapes and sizes also work perfectly well. Half-barrels, cast-off bathtubs, galvanized washtubs and big canning kettles will all hold a plant or more and may be attractive enough to take a place in the garden un-camouflaged, as does the Heyd and Santos trough. Sinks and laundry tubs, their drain holes securely plugged, are less attractive but can be sunk into the ground in the manner of any pond or left above ground and surrounded with rim-high annual or perennial flowers. If you sink a tub into the ground, make sure the tub edge extends about two inches above the soil surface so that runoff water will not contaminate the pond. This rim can be hidden under stones or concrete.

Container Variations

Several variations on the theme of container water gardening came to the attention of the editors of *Harrowsmith* a few years ago, when the magazine held a container-garden contest. One contest regulation stipulated that the container had to be portable, and the tiny ponds that entrants described along with the usual window-box petunias and hanging-basket geraniums fulfilled that requirement at least when empty, if not when full. One such entry came from Patricia DeBruyne of Simcoe, Ontario, who lined a wooden half-barrel with plastic, filled it with water and, on the traditional May 24 planting weekend, set into it a very untraditional water hyacinth and a pink lotus that she had planted in a half-bushel plastic container.

William Procter of Penticton, British Columbia, cut a scrubbed 45-gallon plas-

When selecting species for a container gar-
den, keep in mind both the needs and grow- *ing habits of the plants as well as the size and*
location of the miniature water garden.

tic barrel in half with a utility knife and sprayed the barrel with red-oxide primer paint to resemble terra cotta. He situated the barrel in full sun and, when the water had warmed, immersed in it a pink water lily already planted in a two-gallon black-plastic nursery pot. Within a month, the lily began to bloom. As well as barrels, the entrants also used boxes, cauldrons, bathtubs and homemade concrete enclosures to hold their water plants.

What is important in choosing a container is appearance, watertightness – real or potential – and size. As Richardson Wright wrote in *The Practical Book of Outdoor Flowers* in 1924, "The idea that you have to provide water lilies with a pond to grow them successfully is an extravagant and erroneous notion. You can make a great number of them thrive in a half-barrel filled with water." One hardy dwarf lily requires about four inches of soil beneath it – roughly a cubic foot in total –

and eight inches of water above its crown, modest needs that can be satisfied by even a sink or canning kettle.

One must be realistic, however, not only in choosing the container but also in selecting the plants for it. Water-garden catalogues are very tempting, with their full-colour illustrations of lilies in glorious bloom. It is a common and expensive mistake to put too many plants in a pond, a mistake compounded by the spatial limitations of a container. Water plants grow surprisingly quickly and will crowd one another out if overplanted, presenting a sad picture of starving leaves and few or no flowers by late summer. The rule of thumb is that for every square yard of pond surface, you can plant one hardy water lily and four to six bunches of oxygenating grasses, the latter about a foot deeper. A lotus can be grown instead of one or two lilies. If you wish, you can add a dozen scavengers (snails, tadpoles or 43

Water lilies can take up a remarkable amount of space. For example, a full-sized bathtub can comfortably accommodate no more than two hardy lily plants.

freshwater clams) and a fish or two—roughly one inch of fish for every five gallons of water.

In the smallest containers—anything less than 18 inches across—you will have to forgo most water lilies and lotuses, but you could try a hardy dwarf lily or an assortment of attractive water grasses and foliage plants. A half-barrel will accommodate one hardy lily with a few accessory plants. A bathtub has enough room for two lilies, each of which should be planted in its own submerged pot. Before

you start ordering plants, then, measure your container and make sure it is suitable for your needs. One way to increase your options for flowering plants is to have more than one container, as William Procter did: "As the barrel was cut exactly in half, we made a second tub by tightly closing the plugs and planted a yellow water lily in it. Both containers have at least one flower open every day."

Heyd and Santos have another miniature water garden in addition to their trough—an old cast-iron pot about three feet wide and just over a foot deep. The container – also an auction purchase, this one for $4 – sits in full sun in front of a raised bed of annuals and perennials.

"Since water in metal heats rapidly in the sun, we thought it would be ideal for a heat-loving plant. We chose a plant native to hot places, the East Indian lotus *Nelumbo nucifera*. We have oxygenating plants growing in three inches of soil on the outside rim at the bottom of the container and water lettuce and water hyacinth around the edge, floating at the top. The lotus itself is planted in a 10-inch plastic tub positioned on bricks in the centre of the pot."

Plant Choice

Among the most popular flowering plants for all water gardens are water lilies *(Nymphaea* spp) and lotuses *(Nelumbo* spp), both of which have submerged rhizomes, big leaves and showy flowers. Water lilies will bloom throughout the summer until the first frost, each flower lasting about three days. If the lotus has the right conditions of warmth, sun and fertility, it will bloom from early July until frost, leaving behind very decorative seed heads for winter bouquets.

There are now hundreds of cultivars of *Nymphaea*. They can be divided into two groups, hardy and tropical, which are quite different in growth and requirements. Both have the typical round, floating leaves most people associate with water lilies, but the hardy varieties have smaller flowers and smooth-edged leaves, and they bloom only by day, closing at night. The tropicals have indented leaf edges, and some are night bloomers – exotic guests for summer-evening parties. Hardy water lilies, whose flowers usually float, are the easiest to grow and can be kept from year to year if their roots are protected from freezing. In some of the milder northern areas, they can be left outdoors all year. Tender lilies,

Water-loving reeds and grasses beautify bogs and shallow containers.

however, which hold their big flowers above the water on erect, stiff stems, must be either treated as annuals or over-wintered indoors.

Because the hardy lilies are smaller in both leaf and flower, they are better choices for containers (a single tropical can cover 16 to 25 square feet of water surface in a summer). The smallest of the hardy lilies, the pygmies, or dwarfs, are the best of all for containers, as they occupy a surface area of only a foot or two across. They have leaves as wide as four 45

A half-barrel acts as home to the lovely 'Angel Wings' white lotus.

inches and flowers two inches wide or smaller, in white, yellow, pink, red and bicolour. The foliage may be all green or marbled with white.

Dwarfs include 'Pygmaea Helvola,' or 'Yellow Pygmy,' with mottled leaves and small, yellow flowers; the white 'Pygmaea Alba' ('Laydekeri Alba'); and 'Aurora,' which opens yellow and turns orange and then red as it matures. Larger but also excellent for tubs are any of the selections listed as hardy lilies in water-garden catalogues (see Sources). Some of the best, for instance, are the prized Marliac lilies, hybrids of different parentage developed a century ago by Bory Latour-Marliac of France, who helped spark the present interest in water gardening. He produced about 70 hardy cultivars, many of which have not been surpassed. They include the yellow-blooming 'Chromatella,' or 'Golden Cup'; 'Marliacea Carnea,' which has aromatic deep rose flowers; and the fragrant white 'Marliacea Albida,' or 'Marliac White.' This last is recommended by container gardener Judith E. Hillstrom in the Brooklyn Botanic Garden guide *Water Gardening* (see Sources): "In choosing your first hardy water lily, the 'Marliac White' is the easiest to grow and longest-lived; mine has survived more than two decades." Lois Muir of Saint John, New Brunswick, grows 'Chromatella,' which has three-to-six-inch bright yellow flowers and mottled leaves, in a homemade, 18-inch-deep container made of concrete and chicken wire.

Check catalogue descriptions for cultivars for small pools or containers. For instance, the Lilypons Water Gardens catalogue describes the hardy red 'Gloriosa' as "good in tubs and small ponds." In a half-bushel plastic container inside a big metal tub, Patricia DeBruyne grows 'Gloriosa,' whose flowers stay open later in the day than those of most other hardy lilies. DeBruyne has overwintered the rhizomes for three years, and still the water lily blooms profusely every summer, sometimes bearing six flowers at once.

A lotus, too, will thrive in a warm tub. "The first few leaves float on the surface," says DeBruyne, "and then the rest of the leaves stand upright on long stems. The flowers are held above the leaves. It is an exciting plant to watch, as new leaves appear every couple of days." Heyd says, "We chose the white-flowered 'Chawan Basu,' which is semidwarf and ideal for a confined space such as our old pot. The surface of the leaves has a waxy coating that makes any water droplets that stay on them run about like quicksilver. The tuber can be overwintered in conditions similar to, if slightly damper than, those for a dahlia tuber." Within the next few years, much smaller species of lotus will appear on the market. Carole Reimer of Reimer Waterscapes says her company is now trying some Chinese types "so small they can be grown in a teacup."

Other floating plants for the container

Iris species such as Iris kaempferi *are well suited to homemade bog gardens.*

a central stem, and sagittaria, with broad, grasslike leaves, "filter water beautifully," says Heyd.

Many unconventional plants can also find a place in a water garden. Bruce Miller of White Lake, Ontario, wanted an indoor water container with a fountain and chose to grow a houseplant hydroponically – in this case, a weeping fig *(Ficus benjamina)*, which he knew to be a good candidate for hydroponic culture. He planted the weeping fig in its own plastic pot and set it and the smallest submersible pump he could buy into a galvanized washtub about two feet square. The tub was camouflaged within a homemade wooden box, and Miller is now treated to the soothing sound of splashing water. The fig grows indoors in a bright, sunny place in winter, then moves outdoors to deep shade for the summer.

Unconventional plant choices were also made by Roslyn E. Duffus of Waverley, Nova Scotia, whose tiny, handmade bog of native plants floats on a nearby lake. Among Duffus' plants, which she salvaged from a roadway under construction ("and since I am very fond of the lovely flowers of the bog, I had no qualms about doing some transplanting"), are blue flags *(Iris versicolor)*, pitcher plants *(Sarracenia purpurea)*, sundew *(Drosera rotundifolia)*, rhodora *(Rhododendron canadense)*, Labrador tea *(Ledum groenlandicum)* and various mosses, horsetails, rushes and lichens. Duffus says, "I was planning to build a loon-nesting platform in a few years and wanted to see what plants could be transplanted and how much flotation was needed for the weight."

The container, made of 2-by-6 cedar about three feet long and two feet wide, has a base of quarter-inch galvanized hardware cloth attached with galvanized roofing nails. Flotation is provided by wide strips of two-inch Styrofoam wired to the hardware cloth, and there are two wooden skids to allow easy haul-out.

The growing medium is predominantly 47

garden are described in Chapter Five. Some are shallow-water plants, whose roots need to be just an inch or two below the surface. One advantage of the minipond is that plants such as these, which usually spread quickly, can be scooped out easily when they threaten to dominate the container. Water hyacinth *(Eichhornia crassipes)*, for instance, "multiplies rapidly," says DeBruyne, "and many are discarded throughout the season." Keeping company with DeBruyne's 'Gloriosa' water lily is a four-leaf water clover *(Marsilea quadrifolia)*, whose brightly patterned, variegated foliage grows rapidly even though she planted it in a small pot to curtail its growth. DeBruyne keeps it, too, rigorously trimmed back.

"The really important thing is oxygenating plants," says Heyd. "They make or break a water garden." Oxygenating plants prevent algae from clouding the water. Elodea, with its fine, clustered leaves on

The common but always welcome marsh marigold (Caltha palustris) *will brighten up any bog garden with its cheerful, long-lasting spring blooms of brilliant yellow.*

peat moss with compost and a bit of builder's sand added. "My planter generally resides on the lakeshore and gets slipped into the water when it is calm," says Duffus.

Setting Up

Do not fill a wooden container directly, as preservatives in the wood can kill the plants, and unpreserved wood will rot. Scrub and rinse the container thoroughly, ensure that it is watertight, and if neces-sary, line it with polyethylene or a special pool liner pleated to fit. Pour in the soil and water, then trim the top edge of the lining so that it does not stick up above the edge of the container. Place the container in a sunny spot in the garden – water lilies need at least four hours of direct sun daily to bloom, and a full day's sun is best of all.

Be sure that the minipond is easily accessible, as you will be topping up the water every few days. The pot should be perfectly level, which may require shims of wood or slender stones; a water surface

tub is a potential danger. Laws about fencing swimming pools are now common in North America, but garden pools may slip through the legal loopholes.

Fencing the entire yard or deck or installing a decorative fence around the pool alone will increase safety. In *Garden Pools, Large and Small*, authors Leonidas W. Ramsey and Charles H. Lawrence propose another solution: a horizontal grid of half-inch pipe that fits just inside the pond. It must be supported on a sturdy, upright framework that holds it securely three inches below the water's surface, where it cannot be seen except from directly overhead. "The finished results will be most satisfactory from both utilitarian and artistic standpoints," write the authors.

Jane Good of Camden East, Ontario, planted raised beds of impatiens around her two cast-iron bathtub water gardens. Around the flowerbeds went a ring of stones "so that you have to step up. An adult can see over the impatiens into the tub, but a child would be reluctant to step into the flowerbed." Good says that it is important to situate the water garden where it can be seen from the house and from all areas of the yard. Nevertheless, she adds, "Nothing is as good as constant supervision. You have to be so prudent."

Consider the container water garden not as just a horticultural experiment but as an integral part of your entire landscape design. A slightly elevated site shows off plants well – a deck or a place within a larger raised garden bed can be ideal. A rock garden or a somewhat austere corner can come alive with the beauty of a blooming water lily. Tiny ponds are also well suited to a position in front of a garden arch, under a pergola or right at the centre of a herb garden where intersecting paths meet. Even a spot indoors can be home to a small water garden, provided you are not growing sun-loving plants such as water lilies and lotuses. Consider, too, a balcony or south-facing porch. For her downtown Toronto balcony, Catherine Shadd centred

that is sloped in relation to its container is not appealing. Do not place the container directly on the lawn, or you will have season-long clipping chores to compensate for the limitations of the mower and a dead spot of grass at the end of the summer. Also, stay away from places directly under trees, not only because of the shade but also because fallen leaves and needles will foul the water.

An in-ground pool is a hazard for small children – and indeed for anyone, if it is poorly positioned. Even an aboveground

An old wooden trough, reclaimed and water-proofed, can be a beautiful garden site.

mixture of two parts rich, sieved topsoil and one part well-composted cow manure, pressing it down firmly. Before pill-form chemical fertilizers were available, garden guides suggested that the soil for water lilies be amended not only with manure but also with blood meal, one quart to a bushel of manure/soil mix. Later in the season, a couple of tablespoonfuls of blood meal in a small paper bag could be poked in under the roots of a lily whose flowering was flagging—lilies and lotuses are heavy feeders. In keeping with the times, however, DeBruyne fertilizes her 'Gloriosa' water lily with purchased fertilizer tablets a couple of times each summer. Heyd and Santos put a tablet into the soil around the blooming plants every three weeks. Other water plants should be planted in ordinary heavy garden soil and should require no fertilizing.

These other plants, too, can be planted directly in the container soil, as Heyd and Santos did around the potted lotus in their cast-iron pot. In more complex plantings, each item should have its own pot within the larger container. Some plants need to have their roots just an inch or two below the surface, so if the container is deeper, they will need their own pots that sit on rocks or bricks. This can, however, lead to problems with awkwardly shaped spaces. DeBruyne says that because there was not enough room left in her container for a pot of parrot's feather—a plant with vines that trail over the edge of the barrel—she filled a small plastic bag with soil, sealed it with staples and planted the cuttings in small holes in the plastic bag. "I was then able to fit the plastic bag between the side of the barrel and the plastic tub holding the water lily. It worked!"

Hardy lilies have elongated rhizomes, while their tropical counterparts have round tubers. Plant both with the crown slightly above the soil surface. Pour in an inch of coarse pea gravel, and fill to the top of the container with fresh water. The brittle roots of lotus, which resemble a

a bucket of water containing a recirculating pump in a half-barrel of soil. She covered the exposed edge of the bucket with rocks and planted flowers in the doughnut of soil around the fountain. Although her plants were not water lovers, this was nevertheless something of a water garden in that Shadd is "privileged to hear the sound of a waterfall 11 storeys above one of the city's busiest intersections."

Tub Horticulture

If you are planting only one lily, you can place it directly in soil at the bottom of the container. Otherwise, each plant should have its own container within the mini-pond. Each lily needs a container about a cubic foot in volume—a handmade box, a plastic pot or a small laundry basket lined with quilt batting. Pygmy lilies, however, can take a six-inch clay pot.

Half-fill the tub or lily container with a

Glazed terra cotta pots are lovely and, for the most part, portable containers. When top- *ping up, make sure the water is the same temperature as that already in the pot.*

string of hot dogs, should be carefully laid at an angle three inches below the soil surface, then covered with about four inches of water.

Throughout the summer, water will have to be added to the containers frequently. Catherine Shadd tops up the water in her balcony container about twice a week. Add water of approximately the same temperature as that already in the pool. Rainwater is a better choice than tap water or well water. A bucket at the downspout of the eavestrough or at a corner of the roof will collect water that is soft and relatively free of contaminants which can harm both plants and fish. If you are using city tap water, let it sit for a day so that some of the chlorine can evaporate. Allow well water to warm to the ambient temperature before adding it to the pond. If you use the garden hose, always check the temperature first. Water in a hose left in the sun can be extremely hot.

Every time you visit the pond, remove any floating dead leaves and other organic debris that shades the plant roots and can give off poisonous substances. Cut away dying and discoloured leaves of all water plants.

In fall, sometime after the first frost but before the water freezes, pour or scoop out the water and pull out the pots of plants – or the plants themselves if they have been planted directly in the container. Wash the soil from hardy water lilies, trim off all leaves and roots, put each rhizome into a labelled, perforated plastic bag, and place it in wet burlap (which must be kept damp all winter) or in a bucket of water that is neither freezing nor warmer than 55 degrees F. Check the bucket every week, changing the water if it seems murky. Label the bag by pinpricking an initial representing the cultivar name directly into it. The roots of the lotus must also be kept from freezing and can be stored in the 51

Containers with a history, such as old whisky barrels, must be washed thoroughly or lined to prevent toxins from contaminating the water and harming the plants.

same manner as hardy lilies.

If the lily has been planted in its own pot, it can be left in the pot until spring. Enclose the pot in a perforated plastic bag to keep the soil moist, and check it frequently throughout the winter. In spring, shake the plant out of the pot and divide it, as described below. Tropical lilies are usually treated as annuals and purchased anew every spring. Bring in any goldfish and keep them in a tank indoors.

Large containers can be left outdoors covered with boards to protect the pool liner from sunlight; smaller ones such as cauldrons can be scrubbed out and put into a basement or shed for safekeeping until spring. About two weeks before the last spring frost, take the rhizomes or roots out of storage, place them in a warm spot and then replant them outdoors after danger of frost has passed. Either plant the rhizomes directly or multiply them by cutting off any extra eyes to plant separately. Eyes are sections of rhizome that have small shoots, leaves and rootlets growing from them. The new eyes should be submerged only about two inches into the water, then gradually lowered as they grow. Most water lilies are hybrids, so seeds collected from them will not produce plants like the parent.

"Very Easy"

Mabel Heyd and Chris Santos are delighted with their foray into container water gardening. "Our two containers are very easy, low-maintenance propositions. All the potted plants are in plastic pots with heavy clay soil and an inch of pea gravel on top. We put a fertilizer tablet in the blooming plants every three weeks. Other than topping up the water level two inches or so every three or four days and taking out the odd leaf now and then, there is little to do. The drought that

In full sun, both day-blooming lilies (above) and the exotic and richly fragrant night- *blooming lilies will thrive, provided the weather is not too cold.*

plagued the rest of our garden was of no consequence to these containers. We have left the containers unattended for more than a week with no ill effects, and I'm sure we could leave them longer if necessary. What I like most about water plants is that they look invulnerable in drought.

"The birds and the dragonflies seem to love drinking from and sitting on our containers. They are also favourite drinking spots for predator insects such as wasps, hornets and beetles, thus increasing natural pest control.

"These containers are a great source of interest for us every day we are in the garden. The birds, the insects, the flowers, the fish, the snails – everything together makes them a centre of activity. We would recommend this type of container gardening for anyone who wants a very lively and easily maintained garden."

Jennifer Bennett, author of *The Harrowsmith Northern Gardener* and a contributing editor of *Harrowsmith* magazine, gardens in eastern Ontario.

Tennyson wrote, "Little flower – but *if* I could understand / What you are, root and all, and all in all / I should know what God and man is." The following list of water-garden plants, compiled by experts from across the continent, does not aspire to such lofty philosophical heights but, rather, presents personal and practical assessments of more than 60 species well suited to a pond environment. The contributors represent different geographic and climatic regions, and their successes and failures vary accordingly – a plant that survives year-round in southern British Columbia may not fare so well in the clutches of an Edmonton winter or in the troublesome freeze/thaw cycle of southwestern Ontario. ✍ Gardeners will find it useful to investigate the comments of the expert who resides in a climatic region similar to their own. At the same time, each of the contributors offers a unique perspective on any given species – one may find a certain plant's hardiness and vigour to be virtues, while another may dismiss the same variety as too invasive. There is always the unpredictable element of personal preference to bear in mind as well. Northern water gardeners need not be discouraged by short growing seasons and long, cold winters. Many of the species in the list that follows perform excellent double duty as houseplants in the winter months; many others are remarkably hardy and capable of 55 withstanding the worst that a Canadian January can throw at them. An asterisk marks the name of the illustrated plant in entries that discuss more than one species.

The panel of water-garden experts comprises: EF: Eva Feuersenger, owner of Hillier Water Gardens, Qualicum Beach, British Columbia – Agriculture Canada climatic zone 8b; U.S. Department of Agriculture (USDA) zone 8. HRC: Howard R. Crum, operations manager, Lilypons Water Gardens, Lilypons, Maryland – USDA zone 7. SS: Sue See, owner/manager of Moore Water Gardens Limited, Port Stanley, Ontario – Agriculture Canada climatic zone 6b; USDA zone 5. Canadian and U.S. climatic-zone maps appear on pages 82 and 83.

The plants in the following list are divided into five main groups. The first two are water lilies and lotuses, probably the best known and most spectacular of the water plants.

The third and fourth sections describe a wide variety of marginal, bog and floating plants grouped according to whether they are hardy or tropical. Although they are less well known to the beginner than are water lilies, they play important roles in the water garden.

Marginal (shallow-water) plants are those that grow around the edge of the pond, with roots in the water and foliage above the surface. Of value mainly for aesthetic purposes, they also provide some surface shade, which helps control algae, and they protect the pond from winds, making life easier for the quiet-loving water lilies. Some of them are particular about the depth at which they are planted; others are not. (The planting depth noted in many of the species descriptions refers to the distance between the top of the soil and the surface of the water.)

Bog and moisture-loving plants grow at the sides of ponds, not directly in the water. While some species are, once again, rather particular, a great many plants in the "Marginal and Bog Plants" sections

will happily perform in or out of the water.

Floating plants, also listed in these sections, are important for providing shade, especially in spring before the leaves of the water lilies are big enough to do the job. These plants, as their name implies, simply float and do not need to be anchored in soil.

Oxygenating plants – in many ways the most important ones in a pond – make up the fifth section of the list. They compete with algae for dissolved nutrients in the water (and win), they absorb carbon dioxide from and add oxygen to the water, they help clean the water of toxins produced by fish wastes, and they provide food and hiding places for fish. Plant them at least two weeks before you introduce fish, or the fish will uproot and eat them. If the plants have a chance to establish themselves first, they will grow faster than the fish devour them. Most oxygenators prefer a planting depth of 18 to 24 inches, although they will grow if planted anywhere between 9 inches and 4 feet below the surface.

Following the oxygenating plants are some brief notes on fish.

Nymphaea spp

(water lily)

Mention ponds and water gardens to most people, and the image that springs to mind will undoubtedly be an expanse of fragrant and beautiful water lilies. Far from being a horticultural cliché, lilies have earned their place at the forefront of the water-gardening picture. The ancient genus *Nymphaea*, whose origins certainly predate those of humanity, evokes a sense of tranquillity as it floats on the calm water's surface. The hardy water lilies offer a wide range of colours and the ability to withstand the rigours of winter. Tropical varieties present a more exotic list of attributes. Their perfume is intoxicating, their profusion of colourful flowers is astounding, and the night-blooming species

56

toria' is tropical, the most famous water lily ever. Blooms at night although not prolifically. Known for its huge foliage. Latticed framework (armoured) under the leaf. Upturned edges.

allow gardeners to enjoy water lilies in the cool of a moonlit evening as well as in the heat of a summer's day.

EF: Everyone loves the water lilies. With their beautiful flowers, available in many colours, they bring beauty to the garden year after year. Water lilies are also wonderful as cut flowers. A few drops of wax in the centre will prevent the flower from closing.

HRC: Unlike most people who make a living at this, I much prefer the hardy lilies to the tropical. 'James Brydon,' my favourite – hardy, deep red and cup-shaped – begins the season in a surrealistic shade of pink. It has a large yellow centre and twice the regular number of petals, and it blooms prolifically. 'Virginia'* has a white star-shaped bloom. The petals are crinkled and appear to be made of tissue paper. At their peak, the blooms can reach 12 inches in diameter. Hardy. 'Chromatella' is cup-shaped, yellow and small, perfect for a half-barrel-sized pond. Wonderful mottled foliage. Hardy. 'Panama Pacific'* is a tropical with large, purple blooms. Like all tropicals, it flowers prodigiously. It is also viviparous, which means that small plantlets form in the centre of its leaves. Most beautiful. 'Vic-

SS: Water lilies are usually the main feature of a water garden, providing continuous colour from late spring until frost. For best performance, grow them in water 18 to 36 inches deep and in full sun. The hardy perennials come in every colour range except the blues and purples. The tropical day bloomers encompass every shade; the exotic night bloomers explode in pink, red and white. Water lilies are also important for the shade their leaves provide, which helps control algae.

Nelumbo spp

(lotus)

The second of water gardening's "big two," lotuses provide a most worthwhile challenge for novice and old hand alike. They may take a year to get established, but if they are treated gently and given 57

width and the blooms a full 12 inches.

The *speciosum* variety is quite probably the same plant pictured in 6,000-year-old Egyptian hieroglyphics. A smaller lotus is 'Mono Botan,' with rosy-red blooms that reach 8 to 10 inches in width. North America's only native lotus, *Nelumbo lutea** (known formerly as *pentapetala*), has a large yellow bloom. 'Alba Grandiflora' is a very strong grower that sports large white flowers with traces of armouring still apparent. Perhaps the lotus with the best reputation of all is 'Mrs. Perry Slocum.' The enchanting, changeable petals first appear reddish and gradually become yellow-white. All lotus blooms last about four days. The warm months are most conducive to prolific bloom, July being the best month in Maryland.

SS: Lotuses produce large, showy flowers that stand well above round, bluish green leaves. Although they are sometimes difficult to establish, they can certainly be winter-hardy in the Port Stanley area. They will thrive in full sun and rich soil. Lotuses spread by means of creeping rhizomes. They can become invasive in natural ponds. Many species are available, from dwarf (18 to 24 inches) to large (up to 3 feet). There is a wide range of colours to choose from – white, yellow, pink and red – and double-flowering varieties are also available.

Hardy Marginal and Bog Plants

Acorus spp

(sweet flag, sweet-scented flag)

EF: *Acorus calamus* is often mistaken for an iris at first sight. Tall, green sword-like leaves, fragrant when crushed, are good for background plantings. Easy to grow. Also cultivated for medicinal purposes. *A. c. variegatus*,* with cream and green striped leaves, is more compact than regular acorus. While it is very showy and hardy, it is slow-growing. Planting depth for *A. calamus* and *A. c.*

lots of sun, they will reward the gardener with magnificent blossoms and leaves that stretch up to 5 feet out of the water, filling the yard with their perfume.

EF: Lotuses in flower are an unforgettable sight. They are spectacular and very fragrant. With a little care, they will grow and overwinter in the Vancouver area.

HRC: At the most recent water lily symposium in Los Angeles, we brought over a Chinese botanist. We in the Western world, who believed there were only about a dozen types of lotus extant, were shocked to learn that the Chinese have more than 200 different varieties in cultivation. This could be one of the most significant botanical finds of the century.

Lotuses, in general, are large, exotic-looking plants. Most people suppose them to be tropical, but they are hardy – so hardy that in a natural-bottom pond, they can spread 25 feet in a year. Such growth could well be considered invasive. The "never-wet" leaves can reach 2 feet in *variegatus*: 3 to 5 inches.

Acorus gramineus, or dwarf sweet flag, is a miniature version. With its slender, almost grassy leaves, it is ideal for a small pool or terrarium. Very hardy. A slender variegated form, *A. g. variegatus*, has silvery striped leaves that add a nice contrast in the small pool. Hardy but also makes a fine houseplant if kept moist. Planting depth for *A. gramineus* and *A. g. variegatus*: 0 to 3 inches.

HRC: Acorus is grown for its fragrance and foliage. For most gardeners, its bloom is so insignificant as to be nonexistent. Hardy in the Maryland area and grows very well all over the North American continent (with the exception of polar and desert areas). The variegated version is superb. It attains the same stature – 3 to 4 feet tall – as regular acorus, and the strength of its fragrance seems to be about half that of regular acorus.

Acorus gramineus is so slow to grow and finicky about its soil that I have been unable to grow it in any acceptable numbers. I have no true practical experience with it. Variegated dwarf sweet flag is a very attractive plant. It grows 10 to 18 inches tall, but it is a slow grower. While variegated acorus grows at about 75 percent the rate of regular acorus, the dwarf variegated variety grows at about 20 percent the rate of the original. This is not unusual with fancier plants.

SS: *Acorus calamus* is best used for backgrounds and edges. Its green, irislike leaves reach 2 to 3 feet in height. Sweet flag is both hardy and vigorous and propagates readily by spreading rhizome. The vertically striped green and white leaves of the variegated form are well suited to edges and accents.

Acorus gramineus looks best in low borders, small pools or container gardens. The leaves are 10 to 12 inches long. Like other varieties of acorus, this one is hardy. The leaves are dark green and form dense clumps. As with most types of sweet flag, the flower of the variegated form is insignificant; the clump-forming striped leaves provide the interest. The leaves and roots are scented, and it makes a lovely houseplant when not otherwise employed in small pools or containers outdoors. It propagates by spreading rhizome.

Aponogeton distachyus

(water hawthorn)

EF: A favourite with its scented white flowers. Easy to grow and hardy. Planting depth: 6 to 30 inches, but young plants should be started at 6 inches.

HRC: A very interesting plant in appearance and habit. The way the plant and the flower array themselves on the water has always intrigued me. The leaves are arranged like stepping-stones leading to a whorl of white petals filled with what looks like caviar. It is one of the first plants up and blooming in the spring, but it disappears entirely in hot weather.

SS: The water hawthorn is most prominent in spring and fall. It is a shallow-water plant with green, straplike leaves on long, floating stems. It produces a double row of white flowers with black centres in spring and fall. *Aponogeton distachyus* prefers cool water and will overwinter in mild climates.

SS: Not really hardy in Port Stanley, but it can overwinter in protected areas. It floats on the surface and spreads rapidly, creating shade to help control algae. It can be invasive and so is not recommended for large ponds. The small, crinkly, green leaves turn reddish in cooler weather.

Butomus umbellatus

(flowering rush)

EF: The flowering rush is a very attractive and hardy plant. Its large umbels of pink flowers make it a handsome addition to any pond or water garden. Planting depth: 3 to 5 inches.

HRC: *Butomus umbellatus* is a very nice and unusual plant with flat-sided leaves. The flowering rush grows reasonably quickly and reaches a height in Maryland of about 1 foot.

SS: In Port Stanley, the purplish leaves have reached 2½ to 3 feet in height. They are triangular in cross section. The flowering rush is a good plant for backgrounds, edges or, when planted in clumps, as an accent plant. In summer, umbels of dainty pink flowers appear atop bold, leafless stems. It is very hardy and propagates by root division.

Azolla caroliniana

(fairy moss, mosquito fern)

EF: *Azolla caroliniana* is a floating plant that forms mats of small, lacy fronds, pale green in summer, turning red in autumn. Not very hardy unless protected in winter. Can be invasive.

HRC: Fairy moss is an interesting plant; it looks like a fuzzy starfish. But all the floating "unit-body" plants are a problem waiting to happen: it's not as bad as duckweed, but I have seen it damage other more desirable plants through sheer weight of numbers.

Caltha spp

(marsh marigold)

EF: *Caltha palustris** is one of the first aquatics to flower in spring. Masses of cheerful yellow flowers are a welcome sight after the winter. Planting depth: 0 to 3 inches. Shorter and more compact than the single variety is *C. p. plena* – a striking plant with double flowers that often blooms twice a year. Planting depth: 0 to 2 inches.

HRC: Difficult to transplant. People love the yellow flowers, but we shy away from this plant because it is very picky about how much sunlight it will tolerate.

SS: *Caltha palustris* blooms in late April or early May here in Port Stanley. The bright yellow, buttercuplike flowers are set on 12-inch-high mounds of dark green foliage, making this a fine choice for borders and edges. A very hardy plant that propagates by root division.

One of the finest marginal plants is *Caltha palustris plena*, which has very double golden-yellow flowers that are produced in abundance. Growing about 9 inches high, it is quite similar to *C. palustris*.

Glyceria aquatica variegata

(variegated manna grass)

EF: A beautiful aquatic grass useful for waterside plantings. It must be kept planted in pots for smaller ponds. Very vigorous grower. Invasive. Planting depth: 3 to 5 inches. Can also be used as a bog plant if kept in check.

HRC: Very attractive clumping grass. Ours grows quickly only when the roots have been established for some weeks; as soon as the weather turns hot, it grows. It does not like to be transplanted, waiting several weeks to perk up.

SS: A good plant for moist soil. The grasslike leaves are striped cream and green and have a pinkish tint in spring. The striping fades a little by midsummer. 61

Manna grass grows quite vigorously to about 2 feet tall and is well suited to banks and edges if spreading does not cause a problem. Propagate by root division.

Iris spp

EF: All irises are very hardy. The yellow water iris, *Iris pseudacorus*, grows vigorously and produces rich yellow flowers and tall swordlike leaves. If you want to hide a corner, this is the plant to do it. Planting depth: 3 to 5 inches. *I. kaempferi*, the Japanese iris, is available in many striking colours. While it prefers plenty of moisture in the summer, its roots must be kept fairly dry in winter or they will rot. Siberian iris, *I. sibirica*, is invaluable for waterside plantings and loves moist areas. *I. versicolor,** a native of North America that is smaller than *I. pseudacorus*, has attractive blue flowers. A real gem. Every pool should have one. Planting depth: 2 to 4 inches.

HRC: *Iris pseudacorus* is one of the best. Most irises bloom from late May to early June for us in Maryland. Most need a steady water level. I've seen *I. pseudacorus* grow on land 2 yards away from water as well as in water over 1 foot deep.

Of the many wonderful types of *Iris kaempferi*, almost all display a bloom of extraordinary beauty – whether striped, solid or mottled. In winter, the majority of irises prefer a lot of water over their roots, but this is not the case with most of the *kaempferi* – they prefer drier roots in the cold months.

The ever popular *Iris sibirica* grows 8 to 12 inches high. The bloom is very dark blue, and the plant responds well to most forms of propagation.

Iris versicolor, a very strong grower, is a lovely light blue. There are quite a few subtle variations of this plant. I have heard from some southern growers that the slime layer coating the rootstock causes an itching sensation, but neither I nor anyone on our staff has encountered this problem.

SS: *Iris pseudacorus*, with its clusters of bright yellow flowers among green, swordlike leaves, is excellent in massed borders and edges. It is very adaptable to different depths of water. Blooms in late spring or early summer. Very easy to grow. Propagate by rhizome division or seed.

The midsummer blooms of *Iris kaempferi* display large-petalled flowers in shades that range from pink to purple. The leaves grow to 3½ feet high. Propagates by spreading rhizome.

Iris versicolor is good for edges and borders and as a marginal plant. The 3-foot-high leaves are more refined in appearance than those of *I. pseudacorus*. The blue, flaglike flowers are produced in late spring. Propagates by root division and seed.

Lemna minor

(duckweed)

EF: Fish love to eat this small floating plant. It can be very invasive.

HRC: Do not put this in an ornamental pond. Contrary to what its name implies, ducks do not eat it. It will invade to the point of covering the pond in a green carpet that will bury and choke all other horizontal water plants.

SS: A favourite snack of goldfish, duck-

weed spreads rapidly, creating shade and providing algae control. The floating plant, with its tiny ⅛-inch leaves, must be controlled if it starts to inhibit the growth of other plants. I would not recommend *Lemna minor* for large or natural ponds.

Lobelia cardinalis

(cardinal flower)

EF: *Lobelia cardinalis** is a very eye-catching plant when in flower. Try to grow it in 2 to 5 inches of water. Its blue counterpart, *L. syphilitica*, is much hardier but not quite as tall.

HRC: A lovely little red flower. Our Texas branch has had more success with it than I have. Nearly impossible to grow (on a production basis) from seed. Temperamental. Likes its light and soil level just so. Although it's a pretty plant, it does not live up to its botanical descriptions. It   63 is not happy by the side of an ornamental pond – it wants to be in a pot on a patio.

SS: *Lobelia cardinalis* is a lovely, showy plant well suited for borders and accents. Bright scarlet flowers blaze above the tall spikes of greenish bronze foliage. The plant grows to 2 feet high. Blooms in late summer. Needs some winter protection.

Ludwigia spp

(water primroses)

The genus *Ludwigia* includes a variety of aquatic and bog plants, some of which are occasionally classified as *Jussiaea*.

EF: The primrose creeper* is a useful plant in an area you want to hide. Its late-flowering habit brings welcome colour at the end of summer and into fall. Planted deeply enough, it will survive British Columbia winters.

HRC: Not very attractive foliage or flowers. It will crawl over other plants and damage them. I would never intentionally introduce this plant into a pond.

SS: Primrose creeper is not winter-hardy in Port Stanley. The plant spreads rapidly, giving shade and cover for small fish. It may require pruning to keep its

shiny, oval, 2-inch leaves in check. The small, bright yellow flowers thrive in full sun. Easily grown from cuttings.

Myosotis palustris

(water forget-me-not)

EF: This perennial aquatic plant, with its light blue flowers, is an excellent choice for the pool edge.

HRC: Some people do not think much of its appearance; others love it. It has grown very well for me in containers. It can be a little invasive for a natural-bottom pond.

SS: The dense clusters of bright blue flowers with yellow eyes appear in mid-summer. Water forget-me-not is excellent for low pool edges and grows 8 to 10 inches above the water. It will tolerate some shade and is easily grown and propagated by seed and cuttings.

Nasturtium officinale

(watercress)

Watercress, which often grows wild in streams and boggy meadows, prefers cool weather. The leaves, if you wish to harvest them, are best in spring and fall.

EF: Well known for its use in salads. Likes to grow in running water.

HRC: Watercress can be a little invasive at times, but it generally behaves it-

self. It prefers cooler springs and streams in Maryland. Most people are not interested in it from an ornamental standpoint.

SS: Watercress prefers cool, slow-moving shallow water. The peppery-tasting, small, round leaves form a dense mat that spreads over shallow areas, providing some shade and cover for fish. It produces tiny white flowers in warm weather. Propagate by seed or cuttings.

Nuphar spp

(spatterdock, pond lily)

Nuphars, which often grow wild, may be too vigorous for small ponds or water gardens. They are likely at their best in larger, natural ponds.

EF: Spatterdock grows wild here in lakes and swamps. Sometimes called the poor man's water lily, for obvious reasons.

HRC: Nuphars put up a profusion of large leaves 20 to 24 inches across. The infrequent blooms are small (about 2 inches across) and yellow. I find the

blooms very interesting, but our customers do not feel they are worth the wait. These plants are of interest mainly to collectors and botanists.

SS: Although they are somewhat similar in shape and growth to water lilies, nuphars will grow in deeper, colder and less quiet water than their look-alikes. With heart-shaped leaves and small, bright yellow flowers, they spread easily by means of thick rhizomes. Planting depth: 1 to 6 feet.

Peltandra virginica

(arrow arum)

EF: While the flowers are nothing special on *Peltandra virginica*, its attractive, glossy, somewhat arrowhead-shaped foliage more than makes up for them. Planting depth: 0 to 3 inches.

HRC: Most folks love the warped appearance of the arrow arum's foliage. It is a bit difficult to harvest at midseason be- 65 cause the roots can travel almost 3 feet into the soil. It is also quite brittle at the base of the "stalk." It is a wonderful and extremely hardy plant.

SS: *Peltandra virginica* forms an attractive clump that is excellent in a marginal planting. The plant has rich green, shiny, veined leaves shaped like arrowheads, and it grows to about 18 inches in height. The greenish white, arumlike flowers bloom in summer. Propagates easily by division.

Pontederia cordata

(pickerel weed)

Although not a showy plant, *Pontederia cordata* has enough attractions to make it welcome in any water garden.

EF: One of the very few hardy blue-flowered aquatic plants. It is 2 to 3 feet tall and has glossy, heart-shaped leaves. Tall spikes bear tightly clustered flowers. What makes this plant so attractive is that it flowers late in the summer and on into the fall, when other bog and shallow-water

plants have finished blooming. Planting depth: 3 to 5 inches.

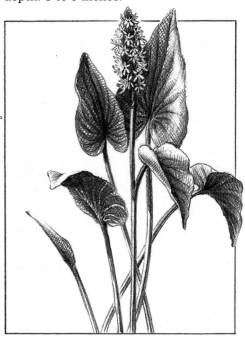

Sagittaria spp

(arrowhead, duck potato)

EF: *Sagittaria latifolia** is a very decorative plant with bold, arrow-shaped leaves. Leaves are narrower and more pointed on *S. sagittifolia*, which grows in shallow as well as deeper water. Some plants here come up from 3 feet down. *S. japonica plena* has attractive white double flowers. Very slow-spreading. Hardy but difficult to find. Planting depth: 3 to 5 inches.

HRC: *Sagittaria latifolia* is known more for its foliage than for its small, white blooms. Very nice, especially in masses. Very hardy. Once it gets hot (July), the arrowhead can double its height here in Maryland—jumping from 8 to 18 inches and more. *S. sagittifolia* is almost identical to *S. latifolia*. In a natural-bottom pond, they can both be invasive, but they are fine in containers. The shape is very interesting—a slim "stalk" flowering into a fatter head, somewhat like a king cobra. *S.*

66

japonica plena has beautiful flowers like small carnations. It blooms a full month later than other spring plants.

SS: *Sagittaria latifolia* forms attractive clumps well suited to borders and edges. The dark green, arrowhead-shaped leaves can grow more than 2 feet high. The three-petalled white flowers are borne on long stems in the summer. It is suceptible to aphids and spider mites. Propagates by onionlike tubers.

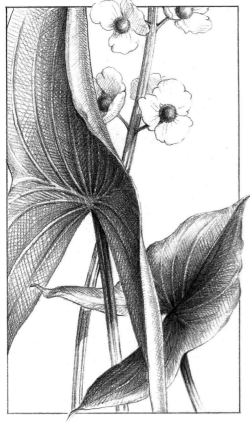

Saururus cernuus

(lizard's tail)

EF: A North American swamp lily with fragrant, graceful, nodding white flower spikes. Should have a place in every water garden. Planting depth: 0 to 4 inches.

HRC: A wonderful bloom—a wispy, trailing tail of white. The foliage looks like something from a creeping vine instead of a vertical plant. When transplanted, lizard's tail takes about twice the time to readjust that most plants do—three weeks as opposed to 10 days.

SS: A marginal edge plant, lizard's tail, with its green, heart-shaped leaves, is attractive grown in clusters. The fragrant flowers are pendulous spikes of white and appear in summer. This 2-foot-tall species grows easily and propagates by root division.

Scirpus spp

(white rush, bulrush, zebra rush)

EF: *Scirpus albescens** is a tall rush with vertically lined stems in cream and green. Grow in containers only. Very elegant-looking. Planting depth: 3 to 5 inches. Also good as a bog plant. *S. lacustris*, with round green stems, is quite appealing when young, but it gets untidy when older. It is very, very invasive and best avoided. Planting depth: 3 to 5 inches. The zebra rush, *S. tabernaemontani zebrinus*, has striking horizontally banded 67 stems in white and green that make it a fine addition to any pool. Best grown in a container. Planting depth: 3 to 5 inches. Can also be used as a bog plant.

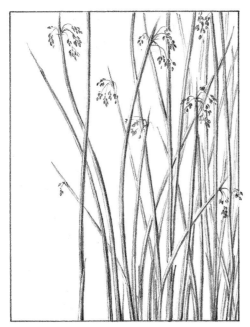

HRC: In this region, if you gather three experts and show them three different types of bulrushes, they will apply the same names to different plants. For this reason, I am shy of the bulrushes. We have three varieties. All are great for pond edges, marshes and anywhere a strong massing clump of vertical plants is desired. Very hardy. I have talked to folks who have no trouble with the zebra rush, but for us, it has been a weak grower.

SS: *Scirpus albescens* makes a very striking background or tall border plant. Its cylindrical stems are vertically striped green and white and grow 3 to 5 feet in height. The white striping is maintained throughout the season. The flowers are small, brownish clusters on the ends of the stems. This rush spreads easily by root division.

The cylindrical green stems of the common, or great, bulrush, *S. lacustris*, can reach 6 to 8 feet in height. It is best as an accent or background plant. Tiny brown clusters of flowers appear on the ends of the stems. Bulrushes can be invasive and should be grown in containers. They are readily propagated by root division. The cylindrical stems of the zebra rush have horizontal green and white bands that are most evident in the spring and on new growth. Small brown flowers cluster on the ends of the stems. Like other rushes, the zebra is best grown in a container. Propagates by root division.

Thalia dealbata

(hardy water canna)

EF: A tall, handsome plant with a tropical appearance. Hardy if its container is deep enough in water to prevent its crown from freezing.

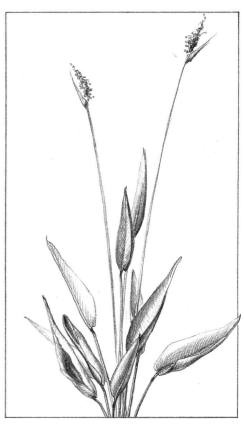

HRC: The hardy water canna is a wonderful, exotic-looking plant that is completely hardy as well. It has neat little dark blue blooms held about 1½ inches above the 3-foot-high foliage. I don't know why it is not more popular among water gardeners.

SS: In mid- to late summer, clusters of purple flowers are borne on long stems well above the green, spear-shaped leaves. Reaching 5 feet in height, the hardy canna makes a striking tall accent or background plant. Easily propagated by root division.

Typha spp

(cattail, graceful cattail)

EF: The cattails are often mistakenly called bulrushes. You either like them or you don't. Its narrow leaves give *Typha angustifolia* a graceful appearance. Planting depth: 3 to 6 inches.

*Typha latifolia** is the giant of the family, for very large pools only. It is invasive and must be grown in containers. Planting depth: 3 to 12 inches.

Typha minima, the miniature cattail, is a very small reed mace that, in the three years I had it, never formed any pokers. Unfortunately, it did not withstand last winter's severe frost. Planting depth: 2 to 5 inches.

HRC: For most ornamental ponds, regular cattail is just too much—too tall, too large, too imposing. The graceful, or narrow-leaved, cattail, *Typha angustifolia*, is a half-scale version, growing about 4 feet tall instead of 8. One interesting aspect of the graceful cattail is that it produces a double catkin.

Typha latifolia is invasive. Give this plant an inch in a natural-bottom pond, and it will take a mile, but it handles itself quite nicely in a container. All cattails look great waving in a breeze. This plant is better suited to larger ponds.

Be careful with *Typha minima*; I have received two different plants under the

same name and was underwhelmed by both. One was small and stayed that way, but it resembled an onion plant more than typha. The other was a small typha that, when given decent soil, became a big full-grown cattail. The true miniature cattail is a painfully slow grower.

SS: The graceful, narrow green leaves of *Typha angustifolia* are very attractive in massed plantings. The flowers resemble slender, velvety, brown pokers. The plants are best grown in containers, as they can be invasive. Reproduce by division of rootstock.

Another tall background plant often used for screening is *Typha latifolia*. The leaves are about 1 inch wide and grow from 6 to 8 feet in height. The thick, brown flower heads resemble pokers. Should be planted in containers. Reproduces rapidly by root division. Excellent for small pools, *T. minima*, the delightful miniature cattail, has slender leaves that grow to 18 inches high. The flowers are 69 short, round, brownish pokers. Reproduces easily by root division.

Tropical Marginal and Bog Plants

Colocasia spp

(taro)

EF: All taros make fine pool plants with their exotic foliage. They grow best in shade. They also make fine houseplants. *Colocasia esculenta* seems to be able to withstand more abuse than the others. But in my opinion, *C. e. violacea*,* the violet-stemmed variety, is the most beautiful of the taros. The dwarf variety, *C. indica*, is the best choice for tubs or very small ponds.

HRC: Imperial taro, *Colocasia esculenta illustris*, is a lovely nonblooming plant. It is very nice in a warm, light breeze but does not like winds. Its maximum height

by season's end in Maryland is 1 foot. *C. esculenta* is almost exactly the same as imperial taro, but most people prefer the darker leaf patterns of the imperial. The bigger they get, the better they look. They can become quite large in the south but do not attain those sizes in Maryland. *C. e. violacea* is a green taro with violet markings. The stems are violet, as are the undersides of the leaves. Sometimes there is a distinct violet band around the leaf edge.

SS: The large elephant-ear-shaped leaves beautifully marked with dark violet make imperial taro, *Colocasia esculenta illustris*, a popular and striking tall marginal plant. It grows to 3 feet tall and can be overwintered as a houseplant. Propagates by root division.

Colocasia esculenta is a tall marginal or accent plant that grows vigorously and produces green elephant-ear leaves. It can reach 4 feet in height and will tolerate some shade. Taro can be overwintered indoors as a houseplant. Multiplies rapidly by root division.

Colocasia esculenta violacea has bluish green leaves with violet stems, making it a striking centrepiece or accent plant. It is slower to reproduce than its relatives. Violet-stemmed taro reaches 3 feet in height and can be overwintered indoors as a houseplant.

Colocasia indica is a small taro variety well suited to container gardens and small pools. The leaves are dark green and grow 6 to 8 inches high. Like the other taros, it can be treated as a houseplant in the winter. Propagates by root division.

Cyperus spp

(umbrella palm, papyrus, paper plant)

EF: *Cyperus alternifolius*,* the umbrella palm, is an old favourite of water gardeners. It looks like a small palm tree. It will spend the winter as a houseplant, but it must never be allowed to dry out. The dwarf papyrus, *C. haspan*, is a good choice

for the Oriental-style pool. *C. papyrus*, papyrus or paper plant, is a tall, stately plant that makes an attractive focal point in any pool. All three species are essentially bog plants, but they can be grown in shallow water as well.

HRC: In my opinion, the three finest vertical tropical bog plants are all species of the genus *Cyperus*. The umbrella palm, *C. alternifolius*, has a tall, straight stem topped by several projections that radiate out from the centre on a single plane. It is really beautiful. The more heat it gets, the taller the plant will grow. I have seen it grow well over 6 feet tall, although in Maryland, 2 feet is about the maximum. It will also survive as a houseplant for a limited time.

Cyperus haspan is built much like the umbrella palm. But the structures that radiate out at the top do so in all directions, forming a little green starburst atop each stalk. This plant, too, can survive indoors for some time.

The paper plant, *Cyperus papyrus*, also known as Egyptian papyrus, looks much like *C. haspan*, but everything is four to five times larger. I have seen numerous examples of this plant in the 8- to-10-foot range in more southerly climes. It bends gracefully under its own weight.

SS: The umbrella palm, *Cyperus alternifolius*, a tall marginal or accent plant, is one of the most popular shallow-water tropicals. A crown of slender, green leaves sits atop the 3-to-4-foot stalk. Tiny greenish brown flowers are found amongst the foliage. The umbrella palm will grow in both damp soil and up to 6 inches of water. It is relatively pest-free and can be overwintered as a houseplant. Propagate by root division or by seed.

The flower head of *Cyperus haspan* is borne on the end of an 18-to-24-inch stalk. Dwarf papyrus is excellent for small pools and will grow in damp soil or 2 to 3 inches of water. Easily grown by root division or by planting flower heads.

Cyperus papyrus is an elegant, airy plant with graceful stems that reach 4 to 8 feet in height. The flower head and a loose tuft of fine leaves sit atop the stems. The tissue of the stems was used by ancient Egyptians to make paper. It grows well in damp soil or shallow water.

Eichhornia spp

(water hyacinth)

Both *Eichhornia crassipes*, which floats, and *E. azurea*, which needs to be planted, are beautiful in the water garden.

EF: A floating plant, the water hyacinth, *Eichhornia crassipes*,* is one of the most useful plants for pools. Its long floating roots filter the water, shelter young fish and provide spawning areas for the older fish. Everybody enjoys its lovely lavender-blue orchidlike flowers.

Eichhornia azurea, the azure hyacinth, needs to be planted in soil. Its beautiful purple-blue flowers are darker than those of the regular floating water hyacinth.   71

In warm, sunny locations, *Eichhornia azurea* will grow rapidly and provide shade, algae control and protection for small fish. It is a trailing plant whose shiny green leaves stand 4 inches out of the water. The bluish purple flowers with yellow eyes bloom readily in full sun. Control by pruning.

Eleocharis dulcis

(Chinese water chestnut)

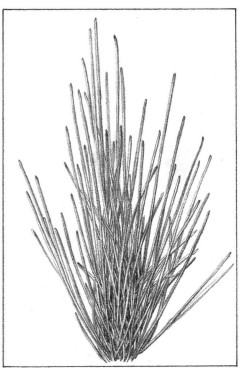

HRC: In the southernmost states, *Eichhornia crassipes* is a terrible problem, overpopulating to the point of clogging waterways. In the north, however, it is topnotch: it fights algae by feeding on the same nutrients; fish can nibble on its roots (it always has enough to go around); it has a nice, light blue flower; and it will bloom with surprisingly little light per day (only three hours).

SS: *Eichhornia crassipes* is one of the best plants for maintaining a natural balance in the pool. It provides shade, and the roots absorb excess nutrients, thus helping to control algae and purify the water. Goldfish use the roots as a spawning ground, and the baby fish find refuge among them. However, large goldfish and koi can cause problems by eating the roots. In Port Stanley's climate, the shiny green rosettes of leaves with spongy petioles are the main features. Purplish blue blooms with distinct golden eyes will appear readily in hot, sunny conditions.

EF: This plant is grown for its edible tubers, not for its beauty. It sends out long, green, cylindrical stems that are very fragile.

HRC: Along with lotus tubers and arrowhead tubers, this is probably the best known of the edible aquatics. Its claim to fame is the chestnut, which is produced underwater.

SS: Chinese water chestnut is a low marginal plant. The vertical, tubular green stems reach about 20 inches in

72

height. Occasionally, flower spikelets are produced on the end of a stem. The tuberous root is edible.

Hydrocharis morsus-ranae

(frog's bit)

Hydrocharis morsus-ranae, which looks like a tiny water lily, is one of the pleasantest of the floating plants.

EF: An attractive little floating plant with round leaves and tiny white flowers. Hardy in mild winters.

SS: Frog's bit is a small, floating plant that will help balance the pool by providing shade and algae control. Its roundish leaves are about 1 inch across. If you have many snails, protect your frog's bit, as it is a preferred snack of the mollusks.

Hydrocleys nymphoides

(water poppy)

EF: *Hydrocleys nymphoides* is a tropical plant well worth having in your water garden. It is very attractive with its large, poppylike yellow flowers.

HRC: The water poppy has small, yellow, trumpet-shaped blooms and an abundance of green, glossy, silver-dollar-sized leaves. This plant blooms more than do most of this sort, and its flowers are far above the rest of its class in both size and beauty. A winner.

SS: *Hydrocleys nymphoides* is an attractive trailing plant that spreads out well over shallow water. It provides plenty of shade for fish and at the same time helps control algae by blocking out sunlight. The shiny, round, green leaves float or stand slightly out of the water. Bright yellow, three-petalled flowers are produced in full sun. Blooms usually last one day. It is easy to propagate by root division or cuttings.

Hymenocallis liriosome

(spider lily)

This native of Louisiana and Texas brings scent and beauty to a water garden.

EF: The spider lily has large, white, fragrant flowers with narrow petals. A tropical plant, but last year, I forgot about six plants and left them outside all winter. Amazingly, they all survived.

HRC: It doesn't grow quickly, but it 73

clusters 6 to 8 inches above the completely horizontal trailing stems, and it has roundish green leaves that are about 1 inch in diameter. Moneywort is easily propagated from self-rooted stems.

Myriophyllum proserpinacoides

(parrot's feather)

EF: Hardy in British Columbia. It's an ideal plant for protecting your baby fish. A favourite here. Everybody likes its delicate, green, feathery stems trailing between the lily leaves and pond edges. Planting depth: 3 to 5 inches.

HRC: This plant does resemble green feathers growing from a common stem, but the parrot appearance is only in evidence above water. The plant has vinelike characteristics underwater, and it can grow for several feet. Contrary to earlier opinion, recent tests show this plant is of no great value in fighting algae or aiding water quality.

SS: *Myriophyllum* is an excellent shallow-water plant that spreads readily. It is ideal for covering the edge of a pool. The feathery green foliage, which adds deli-

grows very nicely. And it has an extremely elegant bloom. There is talk of a much hardier version that is purported to be a native of New Jersey.

SS: Spider lily is an emergent marginal plant with a bulbous root. Its long, green straplike leaves grow about 18 inches high. The large white flower is very fragrant, and it has narrow, spiderlike petals. Blooms in summer.

Lysimachia nummularia

(moneywort)

EF: A hardy, creeping, moisture-loving plant, *Lysimachia nummularia* has small leaves close to the stems and a profusion of numerous (*nummularia*) yellow flowers that are the same size as the leaves. This plant will trail into the water when planted at the edge of the water garden. Grows in sun or shade; prefers a little of each.

HRC: In some areas, we have nice patches, but it refuses to grow in other places. It doesn't transplant well. My hands-on experience with this one is limited.

SS: Moneywort is well suited to pool
edges. The flowers are produced in tiny

EF: This is a lovely little plant. Its white flowers with fringed petals resemble snowflakes. Ideal plant for a miniature water garden.

HRC: A wonderful plant. It has blooming spurts that last about a week. A spurt will produce a carpet of fuzzy, white blooms held about an inch above the water surface. The foliage is pleasant as well. Leaves are heart-shaped with a lighter shade inside the dark band around the edges.

SS: Water snowflake is a shallow-water plant resembling a tiny water lily. The dainty white flowers for which the plant is named are produced in the axils of the 2-to-3-inch leaves. New roots are formed from the axils as leaves break away.

cate texture and contrasts nicely with other plants, provides cover and protection for baby fish. Parrot's feather can tolerate cold water conditions. Propagate by cuttings.

Nymphoides indica

(water snowflake)

Orontium aquaticum

(golden club)

EF: Very attractive leaves. The poker-like yellow flowers are sure to attract attention. Does very well here. Planting depth: 3 to 12 inches.

HRC: Water runs off its leaves like mercury. A yellow, vertical, blooming stem. Prefers some shade in Maryland (al- 75 though it grows in full sun in our Houston facility). Sometimes a little difficult to transplant. Combines features in a way no other plant does. An outstanding plant.

SS: *Orontium aquaticum* produces golden pencil-like flowers on a long, whitish stem. The foliage, composed of long, oval, green leaves, may float or become emergent in shallow water. The strong root system does not transplant easily. Propagate by seed or division.

Pistia stratiotes

(water lettuce, shellflower)

EF: Perfect for shady pools, this elegant floating plant with delicate trailing roots appeals to everybody.

HRC: Some of the large free-floating water plants are quite beneficial to the pond environment, and water lettuce should be one of them. But it falls short in tests I've run over most of the past decade. The problem is that it looks trashy, and its roots are as poor-looking as its foliage. I may get 1 plant in 50 that I feel is decent.

SS: *Pistia* is another genus of floating plant that provides shade and algae control. The trailing roots shelter fish and ab-

sorb excess nutrients. Although the tiny white flowers are not easily seen, the rosettes of velvety, bluish green leaves are very attractive. *P. stratiotes* will tolerate some shade, but it will not thrive in cool water. Propagates by runners.

Salvinia rotundifolia

(salvinia, water fern)

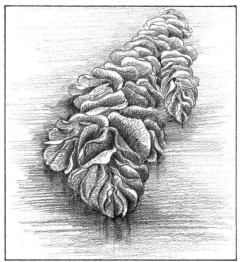

EF: Good floating plant in very small ponds. Perhaps best considered an annual. Does well in shade.

HRC: As with most of the other small free-floating plants, I don't recommend introducing it into a pond, although this variety is quite interesting to study.

SS: This tiny floating plant with trailing roots helps with algae control by providing shade and consuming excess nutrients. The leaves are about ¼-inch across and have many tiny hairs on the surfaces. If salvinia starts to become invasive, you can easily remove it with a net.

Thalia spp

(tropical water canna, red-stemmed thalia)

EF: If you want something big, tall and spectacular, these are the plants to have. Difficult to overlook.

HRC: Lovely plant that gives us a small white bloom each year. It seems to be sensitive to heat. Very delicate-looking and attractive.

SS: Cabomba is not hardy in Port Stanley. It grows submerged, providing oxygen and controlling algae. The light green, fan-shaped leaves grow underwater on stems 12 to 18 inches long. It prefers warm, still water.

HRC: *Thalia geniculata** produces dark blue blooms on spikes well above the foliage. It grows to 5 feet in Maryland — taller in hotter regions. Three seasons ago, Longwood Gardens in Pennsylvania released a fantastic family of canna hybrids with wonderfully exotic-looking foliage and exquisite blooms. Here, they bloom the most in August and September.

SS: *Thalia divaricata* forms attractive clumps and is well suited for a background role or as an accent. The green, spear-shaped leaves are 4 to 5 feet high, and the purple flower clusters appear on stems held above the foliage. Blooms in summer. Propagates easily by root division.

Oxygenating Plants

Cabomba caroliniana

(cabomba)

EF: Should be protected from fish when first planted. A good oxygenator, it is as delicate as it looks.

Elodea canadensis

(elodea)

EF: A very hardy and vigorous plant. Fish love it.

HRC: In my tests, this one is tops. It tends to look a little like seaweed, but it has the most beneficial impact on water quality, which is why I put underwater grasses in my pond at all.

SS: One of the best and most popular oxygenators, elodea is very hardy and prefers somewhat alkaline water. The 77

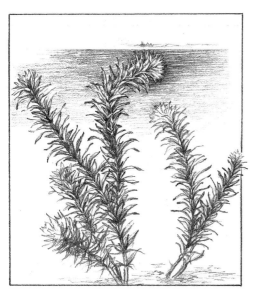

narrow, green leaves grow in whorls around the stem. I would advise container planting, as it can become invasive.

Hygrophila spp

(hygrophila)

EF: Not hardy outside. Good indoor pond and aquarium plant.

SS: Hygrophila is not winter-hardy in Port Stanley. It is an oxygen-producing plant that will grow both submerged and emergent. Thin, green leaves are produced along the stem. It is attractive in clusters.

Sagittaria spp

(sagittaria)

While some sagittarias make attractive and hardy marginal plants, others are excellent for oxygenating the water.

EF: Will carpet the bottom of the pond with grasslike growth. Attractive and very hardy.

HRC: It's the dwarf variety that we use as a submersible grass. It does a good job of cleaning the water, but it is not in the same class as the other grasses. I believe we sell most of ours to people who think the regular grasses look too much like seaweed.

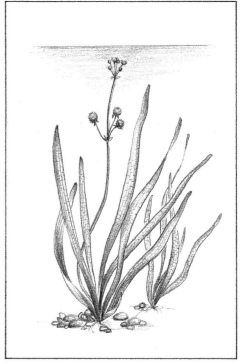

SS: Sagittaria's dark green, grasslike leaves grow 10 inches long and are fine producers of oxygen. Some species send up emergent leaves in shallow water. There is a wide range of sizes and species, some of which produce tiny white flowers with yellow centres. Spreads mainly by runners.

Vallisneria spp

(ribbon grass, eel-grass, tape-grass)

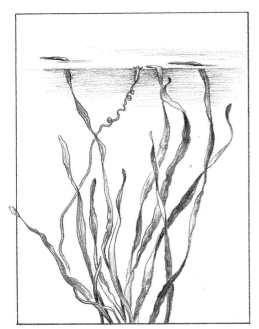

In spite of their common names, vallisnerias are not grasses; they belong instead to the frog's bit family.

EF: Depending on the variety, vallisneria can grow up to 24 inches long. It is an excellent plant for deeper ponds.

HRC: I like this variety better in an aquarium than a pond. It does a good job of filtering the water, probably a little better than dwarf sagittaria. The American and jungle vallisnerias have done a better job for me than has the corkscrew variety. Unfortunately, I prefer the appearance of the latter. All of these grassy plants can be invasive in a natural-bottom pond.

SS: Many species of vallisneria, with their long, ribbonlike foliage, are well suited to both outdoor and aquarium use. The tiny white flowers are produced on long, spiral stems. The leaves grow up to 2 feet long and half an inch wide. Ribbon grass is usually propagated by runners.

Fish

While snails, insects, frogs and toads will all find their way to a new pond uninvited (to be welcomed with varying degrees of warmth), fish are the creatures that water gardeners choose for themselves. Fish are the ones that bring colour, life and grace to the water, not to mention a significant contribution to insect control. They are also the guests that need a little care.

Once established in a pond, ornamental cold-water fish have few requirements — well-oxygenated, unpolluted water, sufficient food and freedom to swim.

Beyond that, care is mostly a matter of what you shouldn't do:
• When introducing new fish to a pond, don't release them directly into the water. They are very sensitive to sudden changes in temperature. Float the bag or container,

79

covering it to keep out sunlight, in the pond water for an hour so that temperature in the bag gradually matches that of the pond.
• Don't overfeed them. Give them no more than they can eat in five minutes. Some feeding is necessary in new ponds, but in mature ponds with established plants, much of what they need will already be there. Train fish to come for food by tapping on the edge of the pool or clapping before feeding them. If, after they have learned the routine, they don't respond, then you'll know that they don't need food. Do not feed fish in winter weather – their metabolism slows down then, and they cannot digest.
• Don't dump anything known or suspected to be poisonous, including alcohol, into the pond.
• Do not overstock, and with a new pond, just buy a few fish to begin with.

EF: The most reliable, attractive and functional water creatures are definitely the goldfish. They will eat, among other things, all the mosquitoes in your pond. Everyone enjoys watching them, and they are very hardy, much hardier than koi.

HRC: Goldfish – comets, fantails, calico fantails, veiltails, and shubunkins – are great. They use little oxygen, school nicely, add depth and motion to the pond and eat any insects that might land there. For the smallest ponds, fantails and calico fantails are the best. Avoid the very fancy varieties.

Koi are strong, hardy and attractive. But I don't recommend them for ponds of less than 300 gallons, as they can grow to up to 1 foot in length.

Do not stock your pond with game fish.

CLIMATIC ZONE MAPS – CANADA

Lower zone numbers refer to increasingly cold areas, but there are no specific minimum-temperature limits for each zone.

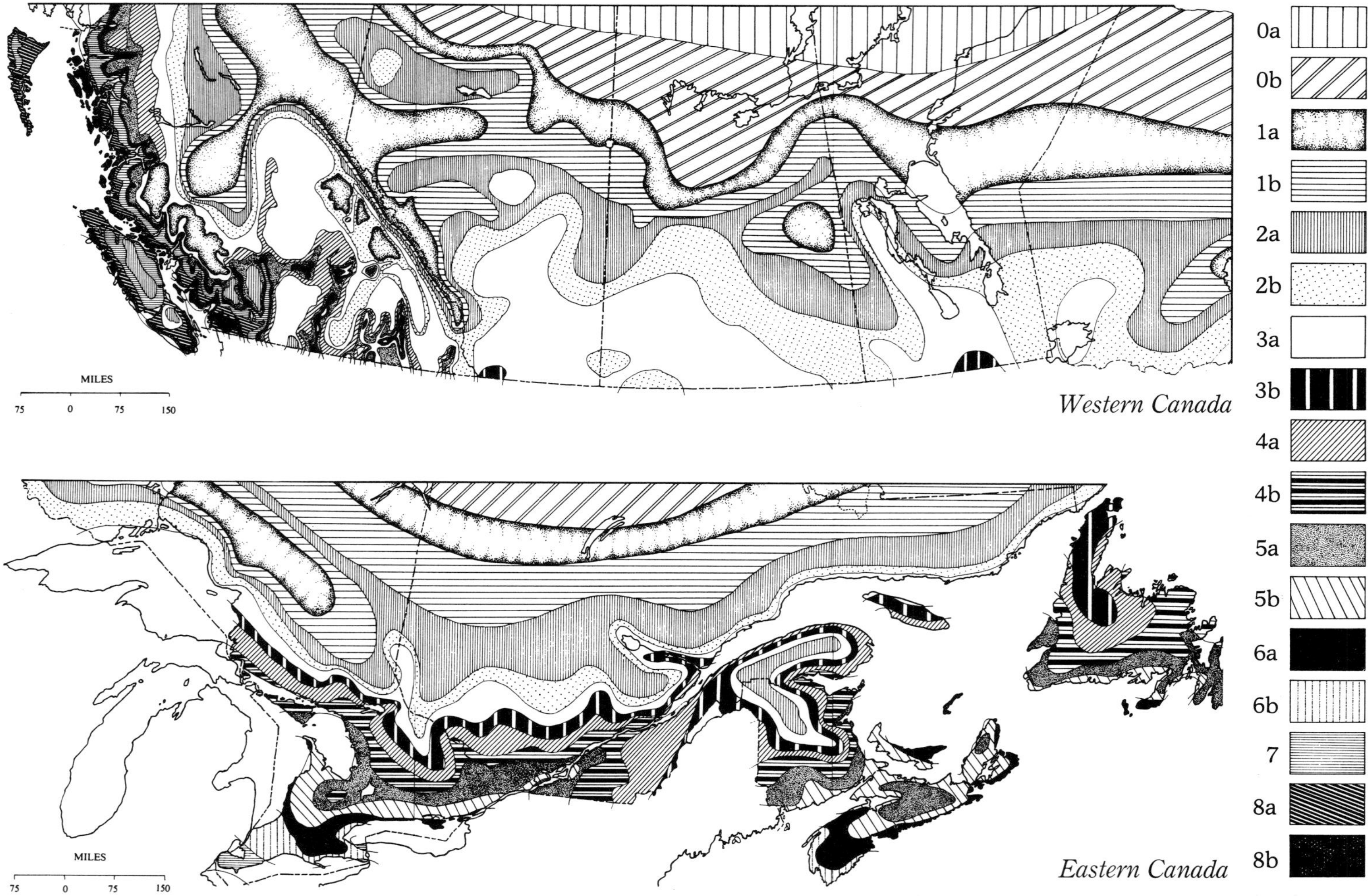

0a
0b
1a
1b
2a
2b
3a
3b
4a
4b
5a
5b
6a
6b
7
8a
8b

Western Canada

Eastern Canada

MILES
75   0   75   150

MILES
75   0   75   150

Average minimum temperatures are listed for each zone in Fahrenheit degrees.

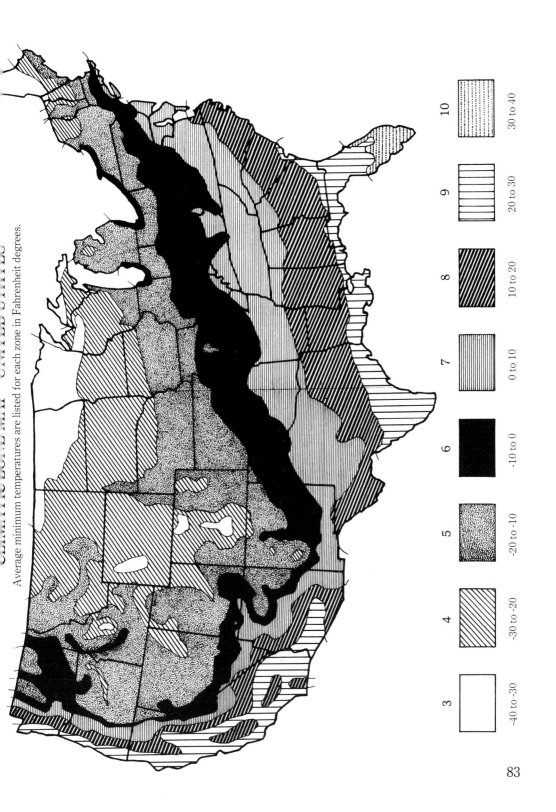

Zone	Temperature
10	30 to 40
9	20 to 30
8	10 to 20
7	0 to 10
6	-10 to 0
5	-20 to -10
4	-30 to -20
3	-40 to -30

Societies

International Water Lily Society
Box 104
Buckeystown, Maryland 21717
(301) 874-5503
For $24 (U.S.) a year, membership includes a substantial quarterly journal, with articles of interest to both novice and expert, up-to-date information on new publications, sources and meetings. The society can also put members in touch with others in their own areas. An invaluable resource.

Mail-Order Directory

Importing seeds usually presents little difficulty, but as plants and roots are fragile, it is probably a good idea to order them from nurseries in your own country—red tape and delays caused by mailing dis-

tances lessen the chances of plant survival.

Canadians wishing to buy plant material other than seeds from U.S. nurseries should obtain a "permit to import" from The Food Production & Inspection Branch, Agriculture Canada, 59 Camelot Drive, Nepean, Ontario K1A 0Y9. Request one application for each company from which you are planning to order plants.

Plant material exported from Canada to the United States must include an invoice showing the quantity and value of the plants as well as a document from Agriculture Canada certifying that the plants are free of insects and diseases. Canadian nurseries that accept U.S. orders routinely comply with these requirements.

Canada

A Fleur d'eau
Stanbridge East, Quebec J0J 2H0

(514) 248-7008
Specializes in growing its own water lilies—many different and new hybrids. Also sells bog and marginal plants, liners, pumps and pool supplies. Will ship to the U.S. Price list containing some descriptions and information $4.

Hillier Water Gardens and Nurseries
Box 662
Qualicum Beach, British Columbia
V9K 1T2
(604) 752-6109
Everything needed for water gardens and more. Extensive selection of aquatic plants. Specializes in water lilies and lotuses. Also books, liners, fibreglass and other pool supplies. Does not ship to the U.S. Price list $2, refundable with purchase.

The Lily Pool
RR 2
3324 Pollock Road
Keswick, Ontario L4P 3E9
(905) 476-7574
Every water plant one could possibly think of as well as pools, pumps, fibreglass, liners, etc. Will ship to the U.S. Catalogue $2, refundable with first order.

Moore Water Gardens Limited
Box 70
Port Stanley, Ontario N5L 1J4
(519) 782-4052
Aquatic plants, full range of water lilies, submersible pumps, fountains, fibreglass, PVC pool liners. Anything needed for a water garden. Does not ship to the U.S. Catalogue free.

Reimer Waterscapes®
Box 34
Tillsonburg, Ontario N4G 4H3
(519) 842-6049
Full range of aquatic plants, 30 tropical and over 50 hardy varieties of water lily and over 75 varieties of bog and shallow-water plants. Specializes in propagating its own plants. Also pumps, liners, fertil-

izers, decorative fountains. Will ship to the U.S. Free brochure.

United States

Gilberg Perennial Farms
2906 Ossenfort Road
Glencoe, Missouri 63038
(314) 458-2033
Full line of aquatic plants—lotuses, lilies, bog, floating—plus a collection of 1,500 perennials, many of which are good water-garden companions—astilbes, irises, ground covers. Does not ship to Canada. Handbook $4 (U.S.).

Lilypons Water Gardens
6800 Lilypons Road
Box 10
Buckeystown, Maryland 21717-0010
(301) 874-5133
Carries everything, including information, needed to build and set up a pond. Operating since 1917. Will ship to Canada. Beautiful 76-page annual catalogue, free.

Perry's Water Gardens
191 Leatherman Gap Road
Franklin, North Carolina 28734
(704) 524-3264
Specializes in hardy aquatic plants. Also sells water-garden supplies. Will ship to Canada. Catalogue free.

Slocum Water Gardens
1101 Cypress Gardens Boulevard
Winterhaven, Florida 33884
(813) 293-7151
Carries everything for outdoor ponds and pools. Will ship to Canada. Catalogue $3 (U.S.).

Van Ness Water Gardens
2460 North Euclid Avenue
Upland, California 91784-1199
(909) 982-2425
All plants, hardy and tropical lilies, pool supplies. Will ship to Canada. Catalogue $3 (U.S.).

Waterford Gardens
74 East Allendale Road
Saddle River, New Jersey 07458
(201) 327-0721
Carries everything needed for water gardens. One of the biggest U.S. growers of bog plants and tropical water lilies. Will ship to Canada. Catalogue $5 (U.S.).

William Tricker, Inc.
7125 Tanglewood Drive
Independence, Ohio 44131
(216) 524-3491
Sells a wide range of aquatic plants; 'Victoria' and tropical water lilies are specialties. Will ship to Canada. Catalogue $2 (U.S.).

Books

Garden Pools and Fountains, Ortho Books, 1988.

The Gardener's Encyclopedia of Plants and Flowers, edited by Christopher Brickell, Dorling Kindersley Limited, London, 1989.

The Overlook Water Gardener's Handbook, by Philip Swindells, Overlook Press, Woodstock, New York, 1984.

Ponds and Water Gardens, by Bill Heritage, Blandford Press, London, 1986.

The Stapeley Book of Water Gardens, by Stanley Russell, David & Charles, Newton Abbot, Devon, U.K., 1985.

The Water Garden, by Anthony Paul and Yvonne Rees, Penguin, Markham, Ontario, 1986.

Water Gardening, by Judith E. Hillstrom. Vol. 41, no. 1, Spring 1985 of *Plants and Gardens*, the Brooklyn Botanic Garden *Record*, 1000 Washington Avenue, Brooklyn, New York 11225.

Index

Credits